Understanding statistics
and
market research data

David Mort

Understanding statistics
and
market research data

David Mort

Europa Publications
Taylor & Francis Group plc

Reprinted 2004
Transferred to Digital Printing 2005

Published by Europa Publications Limited 2003
11, New Fetter Lane
London EC4P 4EE
United Kingdom
(A member of the Taylor & Francis Group)

ISBN 0 85142 459 7

Contents

Introduction

Published statistics, market surveys, and market research data are used regularly by a range of staff in government, business and industry, academia, and many other environments, and access to both government and non-governmental statistics and research data has increased considerably with the widespread penetration and use of the Internet. Many UK government statistics, for example, are now freely available on the Internet, and trade associations and other non-governmental bodies have statistics and surveys available on their Web sites. The same is true for other statistical publishers such as international bodies, national statistical agencies around the world, and many private sector producers of data.

As more of us use published statistics and research data, the need for a better understanding of what this data means, how it has been produced, and how it can be used becomes even greater. This is the aim of this guide. It provides an easy-to-use introduction to:

- the main economic, business, and socio-demographic indicators
- the classifications forming the framework for published statistics
- the terminologies and concepts used in published statistics and market research
- the key sources of published statistics.

The guide concentrates on economic, business, and demographic data and the emphasis is on UK statistics and market research, although many UK statistics are produced using internationally agreed classifications and survey techniques. Reference is made to European and international classifications, indicators, and sources where appropriate. It is not intended to be a guide to sources, i.e. published titles, services and databases, although reference is made to some key titles and sources throughout the guide; chapter 6 lists some key sources and publishing bodies for further reference.

Main economic, business, and socio-demographic indicators

The guide explains the main economic, business, and socio-demographic indicators in a series of chapters, and in short easy-to-understand entries. For example, economic indicators such as GDP, prices, and balance of payments are familiar terms to most of us but there are various ways to measure and present GDP and prices, and the balance of payments indicator is made up of various components. In business sector statistics, what is the difference between an establishment and an enterprise, and are product sales different from product deliveries? What is the difference between the resident population and the enumerated population, and how does the census compare with the mid-year estimates of population?

Classifications

There are numerous classification schemes and systems which provide the framework for many surveys and time series. The main UK and international classification schemes are described, including industry, product, socio-demographic, and geographical schemes.

Terminologies, concepts, and statistical devices

An understanding of some key terminologies and concepts is essential if published statistics and research data are to be used effectively. These are described and chapter 7 considers some of the regularly used terminologies, concepts, and devices with examples of how these are used and constructed. That chapter also includes some hints on statistical calculations, such as growth rates and percentage changes, but the aim is to keep these hints as simple and as easy to understand as possible.

Key sources of published statistics

This is not intended as a guide to published statistics and surveys. There are other sources which can be used to trace sources and services, and details are given in chapter 6. However, some key UK and international titles, publishing sources, and other bodies are also listed in that chapter. Many of these titles and sources have been referred to in other sections of the guide. More statistical publications in the UK are being made available as Web pages or downloadable PDF files, and details of the relevant URLs for these publications are given where possible.

Appendices include a list of abbreviations and acronyms, and a selected list of Web sites offering more information on the sources listed in this guide. An alphabetical subject index has details of all the topics and indicators covered by the guide.

Users of the guide

This guide offers support to anyone using statistics and research data regularly or occasionally by explaining specific indicators, classifications, terminologies, and sources in short easy-to-understand entries.

Users can dip into the guide whenever they are unsure about the meaning or scope of a specific statistical indicator or terminology, or are unclear about the nature and scope of a specific survey or classification.

Understanding of statistics can vary considerably but this guide is likely to appeal to a range of users including:

*   librarians and information officers in various sectors, many of whom use statistics regularly
*   business students, other students, and academics using statistics and market research data regularly
*   various levels of market research and other research staff in companies and research agencies
*   an increasing number of non-professional staff, such as PAs and secretaries, increasingly using the Web to find statistics and market research data.

Layout

After a brief introduction, entries in each chapter are arranged alphabetically. Most entries offer a short description. There are seven chapters:

Chapter 1   Classifications
Chapter 2   Economic and financial statistics
Chapter 3   Demographic statistics
Chapter 4   Business statistics
Chapter 5   Market and media data
Chapter 6   Selected statistical surveys and sources
Chapter 7   Terminologies, concepts, and statistical devices

There are three appendices:

Appendix 1   Abbreviations and acronyms
Appendix 2   Selected web sites
Appendix 3   Statistics users' councils and statistics user groups

1

Classifications

Classifications form the bedrock on which most published statistics are based. These classification schemes enable data and survey results to be presented in a logical way. This chapter lists and describes the core classification schemes in alphabetical order with reference to both UK schemes and the major international classifications. More details about classifications used in UK government statistics can be found on the Web at: *www.statistics.gov.uk/methods_quality/classifications.asp*.

Details of the major international classifications can be found at: *www.un.org/Depts/unsd/class/class1.htm*.

Classification schemes attempt to classify such things as economic activities (industrial and sector classifications), products and services (product classifications), people (demographic classifications), the labour market (occupational classifications), and lifestyles (socio-demographic and geo-demographic classifications). Most established official statistical series are based on classification schemes which are revised periodically to accommodate changing conditions and circumstances. For example, industrial sectors that are no longer particularly significant may be removed from an industrial classification and new, growing industries may be added.

There are also geographical classifications which can prescribe the geographical coverage of many published statistics. For example, statistics for the Central African Customs and Economic Union (CACEU) are only likely to cover the six African states that are members. Published statistics for 'Europe' may come in a variety of geographical options including statistics for the European Union 11 (the 11 member states originally joining the EMU), the European Union 15 (current member states of the European Union), the European Economic Area (EU member states plus members of the European Free Trade Association excluding Switzerland), OECD European members, or members of the Council of Europe (41 countries).

In the UK, statistics may be published for the UK as a whole, for Great Britain, or sometimes for England, Wales, Scotland, and Northern

Ireland separately. They are more likely to be published separately in areas such as demographic data, education, and health statistics where the responsibility for the collection and dissemination of statistics lies with individual government bodies in the constituent countries of the UK. Although there are logical reasons for these geographical divisions, it can be confusing for the user to find that one statistical series covers all of the UK whereas another may cover just England and Wales, and another may only cover England. At a regional level, there are also various classifications including Government Office Regions, Standard Statistical Regions, NHS regional office areas, ITV regions, and Tourist Board regions. Statistical coverage can vary, depending on which regional breakdown is used.

Traditionally, most countries developed their own classification schemes and there was little harmonisation between these respective national schemes. For example, most countries have created their own industrial classifications to reflect the unique structure of economic activity in that country and, until recently, there has been little harmonisation of these classifications. This has made it difficult for researchers trying to compare data from one country to that from another as classifications, definitions, and terminologies change from one country to the next. More recently, international organisations such as the United Nations, the International Labour Organisation, and Eurostat (the Statistical Office of the European Communities) have created international classification schemes which are increasingly used to harmonise data collection, analysis and publication across countries and to facilitate more effective international research.

Classification schemes

A Classification of Residential Neighbourhoods

A Classification of Residential Neighbourhoods (the ACORN Classification) was originally developed by the research company CACI in the late 1970s to classify areas according to various demographic, economic, and social characteristics. An ACORN code is given to each Census Enumeration District (ED). There are six major ACORN categories and 17 groups within these categories. The groups are further sub-divided into area types, of which there are 54. The categories and groups are listed below. The ACORN classification is used to identify areas where households have similar characteristics and is used in marketing, market research, direct mail, etc.

ACORN categories and groups

Category A: Affluent suburban and rural areas

>   1. Wealthy achiever, suburban areas
>   2. Affluent greys, rural communities
>   3. Prosperous pensioners, retirement areas

Category B: Affluent family areas

>   4. Affluent executives, family areas
>   5. Well-off workers, family areas

Category C: Affluent urban areas

>   6. Affluent urbanites, town and city areas
>   7. Prosperous professionals, metropolitan areas
>   8. Better-off executives, inner city areas

Category D: Mature home owning areas

>   9. Comfortable middle agers, mature home owning areas
>   10. Skilled workers, home owning areas

Category E: New home owning areas

>   11. New home owners, mature communities
>   12. White collar workers, better-off multi-ethnic areas

Category F: Council estates and low income areas

>   13. Older people, less prosperous areas
>   14. Council estate residents, better-off homes
>   15. Council estate residents, high unemployment
>   16. Council estate residents, greatest hardship
>   17. People in multi-ethnic low income areas

Each group is divided into types, for example 'Wealthy achievers, suburban areas' is divided into:

>   1.1 Wealthy suburbs, large detached houses
>   1.2 Villages with wealthy commuters

1.3 Mature affluent home owning areas

1.4 Affluent suburbs, older families

1.5 Mature well-off suburbs

A C Nielsen Regions

The AC Nielsen regions are: London; Anglia; Southern; Wales, West and Westward; Midlands; Lancashire; Yorkshire; Tyne Tees; Scotland.

ACORN Classification

See A Classification of Residential Neighbourhoods.

Andean Common Market

Andean Common Market (ANCOM) members are Bolivia, Colombia, Ecuador, Peru, and Venezuela.

Asian-Pacific Economic Cooperation

Asian-Pacific Economic Cooperation (APEC) members are Australia, Brunei Darussalam, Canada, Chile, China, Hong Kong, Indonesia, Japan, Malaysia, Mexico, New Zealand, Papua New Guinea, Peru, Philippines, Republic of Korea, Russian Federation, Singapore, Taiwan, Thailand, USA, and Vietnam.

Association of South-East Asian Nations

Association of South-East Asian Nations (ASEAN) members are: Brunei Darussalam, Cambodia, Indonesia, Lao People's Democratic Republic, Malaysia, Myanmar, Philippines, Singapore, Thailand, and Vietnam.

Baltic States

The Baltic States are: Estonia, Latvia, and Lithuania.

CAMEO

CAMEO is a geo-demographic classification system (see Geo-demographic Classifications) for assessing the socio-economic and demographic characteristics of a neighbourhood. Developed by Eurodirect, CAMEO UK divides UK neighbourhoods into nine different groups and 50 distinct types. The nine groups are:

- young and affluent singles
- wealthy retired neighbourhoods
- affluent home owners
- smaller private family homes
- poorer home owners
- less affluent older neighbourhoods
- council tenants on family estates
- poorer council tenants, many single parents
- poorer singles.

Types within each group are given a dual number/letter code, for example:

3 Affluent home owners

3a Younger families in larger dwellings

3b Wealthy older families occupying spacious houses in exclusive areas

3c Affluent commuters in large family homes

3d Wealthy older families in suburban areas

3e Professional couples with school age children

3f Affluent older families in urban areas

Caribbean Community and Common Market

Caribbean Community and Common Market (CARICOM) members are Antigua and Barbuda, Barbados, Belize, Dominica, Grenada, Guyana, Jamaica, Montserrat, Saint Kitts and Nevis, Saint Lucia, Saint Vincent and the Grenadines, Suriname, and Trinidad and Tobago.

Central African Customs and Economic Union

Central African Customs and Economic Union (CACEU) members are: Cameroon, Central African Republic, Chad, Congo, Equatorial Guinea, and Gabon.

Central American Common Market

Central American Common Market (CACM) members are: Costa Rica, El Salvador, Guatemala, Honduras, and Nicaragua.

Central and Eastern European Transition Economies

Central and Eastern European transition economies (CEETEs), often referred to as Eastern Europe, are: Albania, Bulgaria, Czech Republic, Hungary, Poland, Romania, Slovakia, and successor States of the Socialist Federal Republic of Yugoslavia (namely Bosnia and Herzegovina, Croatia, Slovenia, the former Yugoslav Republic of Macedonia, and Yugoslavia).

Central Product Classification

The Central Product Classification (CPC) is used by the United Nations for the collection and publication of commodity production and other commodity data. It provides a framework for the international comparison of the various kinds of statistics dealing with goods, services, and assets. It is broken down into five levels:

- Level 1 – 10 sections represented by a one-digit code
- Level 2 – 69 divisions represented by a two-digit code
- Level 3 – 295 groups represented by a three-digit code
- Level 4 – 1,050 classes represented by a four-digit code
- Level 5 – 1,811 sub-classes represented by a five-digit code.

The 10 sections are:

- agriculture, forestry, and fishing products
- ores and minerals, electricity, gas, and water
- food products, beverages and tobacco, textiles, apparel and leather products
- other transportable goods, excluding metal products, machinery and equipment
- metal products, machinery, and equipment
- intangible assets, land, constructions, and construction services
- distributive trade services, lodgings, food and beverage serving services, transport services, and utilities distribution services
- financial and related services, real estate services, rental and leasing services
- business and production services
- community, social and personal services.

A revision of the CPC is due to take place in 2002.

Classification of Economies

International statistical agencies classify countries and other geographical areas according to their levels of economic development. Typically, countries are referred to as low income, middle income, or high income economies. Another categorisation is developed economies and developing economies or emerging economies. These classifications are used in international statistical publications. The specific classifications used can vary from one organisation to another, but see UNCTAD Classification of Economies and World Bank Classification of Economies for two examples.

Classification of Ethnic Groups

Used mainly for population census data, the Classification of Ethnic Groups is broken down into level 1 and level 2 categories. Level 1 is a classification into five main ethnic groups and level 2 is a more detailed breakdown within each level 1.

Classification of the Function of Government

The Classification of the Function of Government (COFOG) is an international classification that classifies the financial transactions of government for the national accounts.

Classification of Individual Consumption by Purpose

The Classification of Individual Consumption by Purpose (COICOP) is an internationally agreed classification system for consumer expenditure and prices and is used as the basis for many consumer spending and price statistics. COICOP* is the UK adopted version of the international classification.

Classification of Local and Health Authorities of Great Britain

A classification which can be used in marketing, data-profiling, and monitoring. The classification was revised in 1999 to allow for changes in the number and structure of local and health authorities.

Classification of Outlays of Producers by Purpose

The Classification of Outlays of Producers by Purpose (COPP) is an international classification used to classify transactions of producers of goods and services for the national accounts.

Classification of the Purposes of Non-Profit Institutions Serving Households

The Classification of the Purposes of Non-Profit Institutions Serving Households (COPNI) is an international classification used to classify transactions of the non-profit sector for the national accounts.

Classification of Types of Construction

The Classification of Types of Construction (CC) is a Eurostat classification used in the compilation of building and construction statistics.

Combined Nomenclature

The Combined Nomenclature (CN) is an international trade classification scheme used in the European Union and it is a more detailed version, with more product headings, of the Harmonised Commodity Description and Coding System (see separate entry).

Commodity Classification for Transport Statistics in Europe

The Commodity Classification for Transport Statistics in Europe is a classification devised by the United Nations Economic Commission for Europe (UN/ECE).

Common Market for Eastern and Southern Africa

Common Market for Eastern and Southern Africa (COMESA) members are: Angola, Burundi, Comoros, Democratic Republic of the Congo, Djibouti, Egypt, Eritrea, Ethiopia, Kenya, Madagascar, Malawi, Mauritius, Namibia, Rwanda, Seychelles, Sudan, Swaziland, Uganda, United Republic of Tanzania, Zambia, and Zimbabwe.

Commonwealth of Independent States

Commonwealth of Independent State (CIS) members are: Armenia, Azerbaijan, Belarus, Georgia, Kazakhstan, Kyrgyzstan, Republic of Moldova, Russian Federation, Tajikistan, Turkmenistan, Ukraine, and Uzbekistan.

Council of Europe

There are 41 member countries of the Council of Europe usually included in the Council's statistical publications: Albania, Andorra, Austria, Belgium, Bulgaria, Croatia, Cyprus, Czech Republic, Denmark, Estonia, Finland, France, Georgia, Germany, Greece, Hungary, Iceland, Ireland, Italy, Latvia, Liechtenstein, Lithuania, Luxembourg, Malta, Moldova, Netherlands, Norway, Poland, Portugal, Romania, Russian Federation, San Marino, Slovak Republic, Slovenia, Spain, Sweden, Switzerland, the former Yugoslav Republic of Macedonia, Turkey, Ukraine, and UK.

Customs Cooperation Council Nomenclature

The Customs Cooperation Council Nomenclature (CCCN), sometimes referred to as the Brussels Nomenclature, was a classification for external product trade data developed by Eurostat which has now been superseded by the Harmonised Commodity Description and Coding System and Combined Nomenclature (see these entries).

Developed Economies

Developed economies include: Europe (excluding the European transition economies), Canada, USA, Japan, Australia, and New Zealand.

Developing Economies

Developing economies are: Africa, Asia and the Pacific (excluding Japan, Australia, New Zealand and the member states of the Commonwealth of Independent States in Asia), Latin America, and the Caribbean.

Eastern and Southern Asia

In international statistical publications, the geographical area Eastern and Southern Asia includes all developing economies in Asia except those in Western Asia. Major countries included are: Bangladesh, China, India, Republic of Korea, Malaysia, Nepal, Pakistan, Singapore, Sri Lanka, and Taiwan.

Economic Community of West African States

Economic Community of West African States (ECOWAS) members are: Benin, Burkina Faso, Cape Verde, Côte d'Ivoire, Gambia, Ghana, Guinea, Guinea-Bissau, Liberia, Mali, Mauritania, Niger, Nigeria, Senegal, Sierra Leone, and Togo.

Environment Agency Regions

Environment Agency regions in England and Wales are: South Western, Southern, Thames, Anglian, Welsh, Midlands, North West, and North

East. Other regional classifications include government office regions, standard statistical regions, NHS regional office areas, and Tourist Board regions.

ESOMAR Social Grade Classification

The European Society for Opinion and Marketing Research (ESOMAR) has embarked on a programme to harmonise social grade classifications across various European countries. The EU countries covered are: Austria, Belgium, Denmark, Finland, France, Germany, Greece, Ireland, Italy, Luxembourg, Netherlands, Portugal, Spain, Sweden, and UK. As lifestyles, incomes, and educational levels vary from country to country, it is difficult to develop a classification from an existing national one and the ESOMAR classification is based on the terminal education age and occupation of the main income earner.

The level of household ownership of 10 consumer durables is also a contributory factor in the social class categorisations. The 10 consumer durables are colour TV, still camera, clock radio, electric drill, video recorder, electric deep fat fryer, two or more cars, PC/home computer, second home, video camera.

The ESOMAR social grades are A, B, C1, C2, D, E1, E2, and E3 and, although there are some differences in definitions between countries, the broad definitions are as follows:

A Well-educated top managers and professionals

B Middle managers

C1 Well-educated non-manual employees, skilled workers and business owners

C2 Skilled workers and non-manual employees

D Skilled and unskilled manual workers and poorly educated people in non-manual/managerial positions

E Less well-educated and skilled and unskilled manual workers, small business owners and farmers/fishermen

E1 Mainly poorlyeducated supervisors/skilled manual workers and better-educated unskilled workers

E2 Mainly very poorly educated supervisors/skilled manual workers and small business owners plus very poorly educated non-office non-manual employees

E3   Poorly educated unskilled manual workers and farmers/fishermen

The social grades above are similar to the social grades used in some major surveys in the UK. See Social Grades. Another related entry is National Statistics Socio-Economic Classification.

European Economic Area

The European Economic Area (EEA) consists of the 15 member states of the European Union plus European Free Trade Association (EFTA) countries excluding Switzerland.

European Free Trade Association

The members of the European Free Trade Association (EFTA) are: Iceland, Liechtenstein, Norway, and Switzerland.

European System of Integrated Social Protection Statistics

The European System of Integrated Social Protection Statistics (Esspros) provides a framework for Eurostat and member country statistics on social protection. The Esspros methodology was revised by Eurostat in 1996.

European System of Integrated Economic Accounts

National accounts data published by Eurostat, the Statistical Office of the European Communities, and member states is based on the European System of Integrated Economic Accounts (ESA) which gives common definitions for the national accounts and its various components. ESA is the European Union's version of the United Nations System of National Accounts (see that entry). The first edition of ESA was applied from 1970, followed by a second edition in 1979. A new version – 1995 – has been applicable since 1999 for data starting from 1995.

European Union–11

The 11 European Union countries that formed the European Monetary Union (Euro Zone) in January 1999: Austria, Belgium, Finland, France, Germany, Ireland, Italy, Luxembourg, Netherlands, Portugal, and Spain. They have since been joined by Greece.

European Union-12

The 12 countries are: Belgium, Denmark, Germany, Greece, France, Ireland, Italy, Luxembourg, Netherlands, Portugal, Spain, and UK.

European Union-15

The 15 member states of the European Union are: Austria, Belgium, Denmark, France, Finland, Germany, Greece, Ireland, Italy, Luxembourg, Netherlands, Portugal, Spain, Sweden, and UK.

Euro Zone

The Euro Zone is now treated as a separate region in some published statistics. Countries in the Euro Zone are the 11 original member countries agreeing to adopt a common currency (see European Union–11) in January 1999, plus Greece, which joined in January 2001.

Fuel Exporting Countries

The fuel exporting countries are a sub-division within the developing countries category covering the following countries: Algeria, Angola, Bahrain, Bolivia, Brunei Darussalam, Cameroon, Colombia, Congo, Ecuador, Egypt, Gabon, Indonesia, Iran, Iraq, Kuwait, Libyan Arab Jamahiriya, Mexico, Nigeria, Oman, Quatar, Saudi Arabia, Syrian Arab Republic, Trinidad and Tobago, United Arab Emirates, Venezuela, and Vietnam.

Geo-demographic Classifications

Geo-demographic classifications classify local neighbourhoods according to the social and economic characteristics of the population of the individual local neighbourhoods.

Geo-demographics makes two key assumptions:

- Two people living in the same neighbourhood are more likely to have similar characteristics than two people chosen at random.

- Neighbourhoods can be categorised in terms of the population which they contain and two neighbourhoods can be placed in the same category even though they may be in different parts of the country.

Geo-demographic classifications have primarily been developed by private research companies and these classifications are based on an analysis of detailed population census data, plus additional data from other sources such as credit records, electoral rolls, and market research surveys. The companies offer services for direct mail campaigns, store location programmes, etc. See entries headed A Classification of Residential Neighbourhoods, CAMEO, MOSAIC Classification, and PRiZM.

Government Office Regions

The Government Office Regions (GORs) are South West, South East, London, East of England, Wales, West Midlands, East Midlands, North West, Yorkshire and The Humber, North East, Scotland, and Northern Ireland. Other regional classifications include Standard statistical regions, NHS regional office areas, Environment Agency regions, Tourist Board regions (see these entries).

Group of Seven

The major developed economies, usually referred to as the Group of Seven (G7), are: Canada, France, Germany, Italy, Japan, UK, and USA.

Harmonised Commodity Description and Coding System

Introduced in 1988, the Harmonised Commodity Description and Coding System (HS) is a detailed international trade classification now used by most countries as the basis for their product import and export statistics. The HS includes around 10,000 commodity and product headings and each heading is given a numbered code. The Combined Nomenclature (CN) is a more detailed version of the HS classification used by European Union countries (see separate entry).

The latest revision of the HS was approved in 1999 and is due to be implemented in 2002.

Industrial Classifications

Industrial classifications classify economic activities in countries and regions and are used as the basis for the compilation and publication of statistics on industries and sectors. There are international industrial classifications such as International Standard Industrial Classification (ISIC) and NACE, which are described in separate entries, plus classifications in all developed countries and many developing countries.

In the UK, the classification used is the Standard Industrial Classification (SIC) and this is described in a separate entry. This should not be confused with the US Standard Industrial Classification, which is a completely different classification and not comparable with the UK classification.

Most countries have their own industrial classification schemes, and this can make comparisons of statistics across national boundaries difficult. The international classification schemes are attempts to harmonise national classifications, but few countries have adopted these international schemes in their entirety. A number of European Union countries have revised their industrial classification schemes to conform more closely to international schemes such as ISIC and NACE, but harmonisation across all countries is still some way off. Individual country classifications reflect the industrial structure and profile of these specific countries and this makes it difficult to develop international schemes that will be used by all countries.

Some of the classifications used by European countries (excluding the UK) are listed here:

Austria: ÖNACE 95 – Austrian version of NACE

Belgium: BNL and version of NACE

Denmark: national classification conforms to ISIC

Finland: Finnish Standard Industrial Classification, derived from NACE

France: NAF (Nomenclature des Activités Françaises), national classification aligned to NACE

Germany: Systematik für die Statistik im Produzierenden Gewerbe (SYPRO), national classification with conversions to ISIC

Italy: NACE related classification

Luxembourg: NACE classification

Norway: Norwegian Standard Industrial Classification (SIC 94)

Spain: National Classification of Economic Activities (CNAE)

Sweden: Swedish Standard Industrial Classification

Switzerland: Allgemeine Systematik der Wirtschaftszweige

Inter-departmental Business Register

The Inter-departmental Business Register (IDBR) maintained by National Statistics contains records of all UK businesses registered for VAT or PAYE purposes. The register is used for selecting samples for surveys of businesses and producing analyses of business activity. The smallest unit held on the register is an individual site (Local Unit). One or more local units form an enterprise. A group of enterprises under common ownership form an enterprise group. These definitions are often found in statistical publications.

International Classification of Diseases

The International Classification of Diseases (ICD), published by the World Health Organisation, is used in international and UK surveys to categorise diseases and ailments. Since the beginning of 2001, the UK has been using the tenth revision of the ICD.

International Family of Economic and Social Classifications

The International Family of Economic and Social Classifications covers all the classifications registered into the UN Inventory of Classifications, and this includes all the main industrial, overseas trade, and national income classifications. Details of all the classifications can be found on the UN Web site at *www.un.org/depts/unsd/class/class1.family.htm*.

International Standard Classification of Education

The International Standard Classification of Education (ISCED) was established by Unesco in 1976 and last updated in 1997. It is used to compile international education statistics. It covers two cross-classification variables: levels and fields of education. ISCED 1997 levels are:

0   Pre-primary education

1   Primary education

2   Lower secondary education

3   Upper secondary education

4   Post-secondary non-tertiary education

5   Tertiary education

6   Second stage of tertiary education

There are 25 fields of education (at two-digit level) which can be further refined into three-digit level. The fields are arranged under nine broad groups:

0 General programmes

1 Education

2 Humanities and arts

3 Social sciences, business and law

4 Science, mathematics and computing

5 Engineering, manufacturing, and construction

6 Agriculture and veterinary

7 Health and welfare

8 Services

International Standard Classification of Occupations

The International Standard Classification of Occupations (ISCO), published by the International Labour Organisation (ILO), enables information on occupations to be compared internationally.

International Standard Classification of Occupations (for European Union Purposes)

The International Standard Classification of Occupations (for European Union Purposes) (ISCO-88 COM) is the European Union version of the ILO's International Standard Classification of Occupations (see above).

International Standard Classification of Status in Employment

The International Standard Classification of Status in Employment (ISCE) is an ILO classification of jobs held by persons at a point in time.

International Standard Industrial Classification

The International Standard Industrial Classification (ISIC) is the International Standard Industrial Classification of all Economic Activities developed by the United Nations and used as the basis for UN published statistics on economic activity, industry, and services. There are 17 main sections in the classification denoted by a letter code (e.g. D is manufacturing and M is education) and these are the same as those found in the Standard Industrial Classification (see that entry). Below the sections level, the main components of the classification are three-digit and four-digit industry breakdowns and an example is shown here:

D   Manufacturing

155   Manufacture of beverages

1552   Manufacture of wines

1553   Manufacture of malt liquors and malt

Intrastat

Following the abolition of custom controls and duties within the European Union, it is no longer possible to collect import and export data from customs records. Import and export data for trade within the European Union is now collected using the Intrastat system. Intrastat is linked to VAT declarations by companies and businesses and these organisations are asked to provide details of their external trade on their completed VAT returns. The Intrastat system has thresholds so that only the larger companies involved in international trade have to give detailed import/export information. For 2001, the threshold is £233,000 and any company involved in overseas trade amounting to more than this value must provide supplementary information on their VAT declaration to cover trade information. Most smaller companies are exempt, or have to provide only limited information. Data for imports and exports between European Union countries and non-EU countries is still collected from customs records creating a two-tier system of import and export information for the EU.

Intrastat Classification Nomenclature

The Intrastat Classification Nomenclature (ICN) shows the product classification codes for the Intrastat system described in the previous entry.

ITV Areas

The ITV areas in the UK are: North Scotland, Central Scotland, Border, North East, North West, Yorkshire, Wales and the West, East and West Midlands, East of England, London, South and South East, South West, and Ulster.

Latin American Integration Association

Latin American Integration Association (LAIA) members are: Argentina, Bolivia, Brazil, Chile, Colombia, Ecuador, Mexico, Paraguay, Peru, Uruguay, and Venezuela. LAIA was formerly the Latin American Free Trade Association.

Least Developed Countries

The Least Developed Countries (LDCs) category used in international statistics usually covers the following countries: Afghanistan, Angola, Bangladesh, Benin, Bhutan, Burkina Faso, Burundi, Cambodia, Cape Verde, Central African Republic, Chad, Comoros, Democratic Republic of the Congo, Djibouti, Equatorial Guinea, Eritrea, Ethiopia, Gambia, Guinea, Guinea-Bissau, Haiti, Kiribati, Lao People's Democratic Republic, Lesotho, Liberia, Madagascar, Malawi, Maldives, Mali, Mauritania, Mozambique, Myanmar, Nepal, Niger, Rwanda, Samoa, Sao Tome and Principe, Sierra Leone, Solomon Islands, Somalia, Sudan, Togo, Tuvalu, Uganda, United Republic of Tanzania, Vanuatu, Yemen, and Zambia.

Mercado Común Sudamericano

Mercado Común Sudamericano (MERCOSUR) members are: Argentina, Brazil, Paraguay, and Uruguay.

MOSAIC Classification

The MOSAIC Classification is a geo-demographic classification used to classify neighbourhoods by social and economic characteristics. Originally developed in the UK in 1980, the classification is part of the services offered by business information company Experian. MOSAIC has 58 neighbourhood types under headings such as 'elite professional/educational suburbs, mostly inner metropolitan' or 'new greenfield council estates with many young children'. The MOSAIC classification is used to identify neighbourhoods where households have similar characteristics and is used in marketing, direct mailing, etc.

NACE

NACE is the industrial classification scheme developed by Eurostat in the European Union. See Nomenclature Générale des Activités Économiques dans les Communautés Européennes.

Time Series Codes

Time series in some official statistics databases are given a four-letter code and these codes are also shown for each time series in the statistical tables found in hard copy statistical publications from National Statistics. For example, the quarterly publication *Consumer Trends* has specific codes for each product or service included. In Table 3.2, Household Final Consumption Expenditure on Food at Current Prices in *Consumer Trends*, for example, the following codes are given at the top of each product column:

Code	Product
CEGS	Bread
CEGU	Cakes and biscuits
CEGW	Other cereals
CCRL	Meat and bacon
CCRM	Fish
CCRN	Milk, cheese, eggs
CCRO	Oils and fats
CCRP	Fruit
CCRQ	Potatoes
CCRR	Vegetables
CCEK	Total food

National Statistics Socio-Economic Classification

The National Statistics Socio-Economic Classification (NS-SEC) replaces the previously used classification – Social Class and Socio-Economic Group – and is based on the Standard Occupational Classification (see that entry). The NS-SEC is based not on skills but on employment conditions and relations which are central to describing socio-economic conditions in society. All relevant official statistics should be based on this new classification. The NS-SEC has seven major classes:

1.   Higher managerial and professional occupations

     1.1 Employers and managers in large organisations

     1.2 Higher professionals

2.   Lower managerial and professional occupations

3.   Intermediate occupations

4.   Small employers and own-account workers

5.   Lower supervisory, craft and related occupations

6.   Semi-routine occupations

7.   Routine occupations

There is an additional class – 8 – which is used where possible and this covers those who have never had paid work, and the long-term unemployed.

See other related entries in this chapter, ESOMAR Social Grade Classification and Social Grade.

Net-Creditor Countries

The net-creditor countries are a sub-division of the developing countries group comprising: Brunei Darussalam, Kuwait, Libyan Arab Jamahiriya, Oman, Quatar, Saudi Arabia, Singapore, Taiwan, and United Arab Emirates.

Net-Debtor Countries

The net-debtor countries are all developing countries except those listed in the above net-creditor countries entry.

NHS Regional Office Areas

NHS regional office areas in England and Wales are South West, South Thames, North Thames, Anglia & Oxford, Wales, West Midlands, Trent, North West, and Northern & Yorkshire. Other regional classifications include Government Office Regions, Standard Statistical Regions, Environment Agency regions, and Tourist Board regions (see these entries).

Nomenclature Générale des Activités Économiques dans les Communautés Européennes

Nomenclature générale des activités économiques dans les Communautés Européennes (NACE) is the general industrial classification of economic activities within the European Union. The classification is broken down into 17 general headings and there are further sub-divisions within each heading. While most EU countries have developed their own economic activity classifications to reflect their own industrial and business structures, recent revisions of these classifications have tried to incorporate the NACE headings. See Industrial Classifications for more information.

The general NACE headings are:

A   Agriculture, hunting, forestry

B   Fishing

C   Mining and quarrying

D   Manufacturing

E   Electricity, gas, and water supply

F   Construction

G   Wholesale and retail trade; repair of motor vehicles, motorcycles and personal and household goods

H   Hotels and restaurants

I   Transport, storage, and communications

J   Financial intermediation

K   Real estate, renting, and business activities

L   Public administration and defence; compulsory social security

M   Education

N   Health and social work

O   Other community, social and personal service activities

P   Private households with employed persons

Q   Extra-territorial organisations and bodies

In the general headings C and D, the divisions within each heading are given two-letter codes:

C   Mining and quarrying

CA   Mining and quarrying of energy producing materials

CB   Mining and quarrying, except of energy producing materials

D   Manufacturing

DA   Food products, beverages, and tobacco

DB   Manufacture of textiles and textile products

DC   Manufacture of leather and leather products

DD   Manufacture of wood and wood products

DE   Manufacture of pulp, paper and paper products; publishing and printing

DG   Manufacture of chemicals, chemical products, and man-made fibres

DH   Manufacture of rubber and plastic products

DI   Manufacture of other non-metallic mineral products

DJ   Manufacture of basic metals and fabricated metal products

DK   Manufacture of machinery and equipment n.e.c.

DL   Manufacture of electrical and optical equipment

DM   Manufacture of transport equipment

DN   Manufacturing n.e.c.

In some of the general headings G to Q, the divisions within each heading are given two-digit codes. For example:

I   Transport, storage, and communications

   60   Land transport and pipelines

   61   Water transport

   62   Air transport

   63   Supporting and auxiliary transport activities

   64   Post and telecommunications

There are 60 two-digit divisions. There are further sub-divisions into groups with three-digit codes (222 groups), and classes with four-digit codes (503 classes).Nomenclature of Goods for the External Trade Statistics of the Community and Statistics of Trade Between Member States

The above nomenclature, abbreviated to NIMEXE, was a classification of product import and export data developed by Eurostat. The classification is no longer in use.

Nomenclature of Territorial Units for Statistics

The Nomenclature of Territorial Units for Statistics (NUTS) is a hierarchical classification of geographical areas used in EU statistics and particularly regional statistics. NUTS has three main levels – level 1, level 3, and level 4 – with level 1 covering regional areas such as the Länder in Germany or government office regions in the UK. An additional level is level 5. The NUTS levels (1999) are:

Level 0 15 countries

Level 1 77 regions

Level 3 206 regions

Level 4 1,074 regions (in selected countries)

Level 5 98,433 communes, or equivalents

In use since 1988, NUTS in the UK has a five-tier structure – levels 1–5. Level 1 comprises Government Office Regions (GORs) in England, plus Wales, Scotland, and Northern Ireland. Level 2 includes counties, groups of counties, unitary authorities, London boroughs, metropolitan boroughs in England; and groups of unitary authorities in Wales, Scotland, and Northern Ireland. Level 3 includes counties, groups of counties, London boroughs, metropolitan counties, unitary authorities and local authority districts in England; groups of unitary authorities in Wales and Scotland; and groups of district council areas in Northern Ireland. Level 4 includes individual London boroughs, metropolitan districts, local authority districts in England; individual unitary authorities in Wales; individual unitary authorities or groups in Scotland; and individual district council areas in Northern Ireland. Level 5 includes wards across England, Wales, Scotland, and Northern Ireland.

North American Free Trade Area

The members of the North American Free Trade Area (NAFTA) are: Canada, Mexico, and USA.

ONS Classification of Local and Health Authorities of Great Britain, Revised for Authorities in 1999

The above ONS classification covers local government and health authorities and deals with the boundary changes of 1999.

Organisation for Economic Cooperation and Development

The members of the Organisation for Economic Cooperation and Development (OECD) are: Australia, Austria, Belgium, Canada, Czech Republic, Denmark, Finland, France, Germany, Greece, Hungary, Iceland, Ireland, Italy, Japan, Luxembourg, Mexico, Netherlands, New Zealand, Norway, Poland, Portugal, Republic of Korea, Spain, Sweden, Switzerland, Turkey, UK, and USA.

Organisation of Petroleum Exporting Countries

The members of the Organisation of Petroleum Exporting Countries (OPEC) are: Algeria, Indonesia, Iran, Iraq, Kuwait, Libyan Arab Jamahiriya, Nigeria, Quatar, Saudi Arabia, United Arab Emirates, and Venezuela.

PRiZM

PRiZM is a geo-demographic classification created from two key market drivers – lifestyle and income – which are then overlaid with lifestyle interests. PRiZM is offered by the marketing company Claritas. PRiZM divides postcodes into 60 distinct clusters in 16 broad groups, and a five-character code defines each PriZM cluster. The first and second characters indicate lifestage:

PA   starting out, young singles and childless couples

PB   nursery families

PC   established families with school age children

The third digit is an income indicator:

1   most affluent households

2   mid–high affluent households

3   mid–low affluent families

4   least affluent families

The fourth and fifth characters comprise a unique lifestyle description of the cluster. Some examples are: young married; own four-wheel drive; support national causes; and likely to have club cards.

PRODCOM

PRODCOM (PRODucts of the European COMmunity) is a harmonised product classification used across the EU for the collection and publication of product statistics. PRODCOM has been used in EU member countries since 1993 and it was devised to solve the problem of different member countries using different product classifications for their product statistics. Over 5,000 product headings are included in PRODCOM although some of these are not applicable to every EU country. In the UK, PRODCOM has 4,500 product categories in 250 industries. The PRODCOM product classification is based on the product classification used in the Harmonised Commodity Description and Coding System (HS) – the 5,000 plus PRODCOM product headings are headings taken from the HS system. This means that not only is it possible to compare product data from one EU country to the next, it is also possible to match these domestic product statistics with import and export statistics for the same product heading. The PRODCOM Inquiry (see chapter 6) is conducted quarterly and annually in the UK.

PRODCOM is broken down into the following levels:

Level 1 23 divisions identified by two-digit code

Level 2 250 classes identified by four-digit code

Level 3 1,400 sub-categories identified by six-digit code

Level 4 5,800 individual product headings identified by eight-digit code

The PRODCOM divisions, corresponding to the NACE divisions, are:

13 Mining of metal ores

14 Other mining and quarrying

15 Manufacture of food products and beverages

16 Manufacture of tobacco products

17 Manufacture of textiles

18 Manufacture of wearing apparel; dressing and dyeing of fur

19 Tanning and dressing of leather; manufacture of luggage, hand-bags, saddlery, harness and footwear

20 Manufacture of wood and of products of wood and cork, except furniture; manufacture of articles of straw and plaiting materials

21 Manufacture of pulp, paper and paper products

22 Publishing, printing and reproduction of recorded media

24 Manufacture of chemicals and chemical products

25 Manufacture of rubber and plastic products

26 Manufacture of other non-metallic mineral products

27 Manufacture of basic metals

28 Manufacture of fabricated metal products, except machinery and equipment

29 Manufacture of machinery and equipment n.e.c.

30 Manufacture of office machinery and equipment

31 Manufacture of electrical machinery and apparatus n.e.c.

32   Manufacture of radio, television and communication equipment and apparatus

33   Manufacture of medical, precision and optical instruments, watches and clocks

34   Manufacture of motor vehicles, trailers and semi-trailers

35   Manufacture of other transport equipment

36   Manufacture of furniture; manufacturing n.e.c.

The PRODCOM List (see chapter 6) is published annually.

Sagacity Life Cycle Groupings

The basic philosophy behind the Sagacity Life Cycle Groupings is that people have different aspirations and behaviour patterns as they go through the life cycle. The groupings identify four main stages of life cycle and these are then sub-divided by income and occupation groups. The groupings have been developed by research company IPSOS-RSL.

The four life cycles are:

* dependent – mainly under 24s, living at home or full-time student

* pre-family – under 35s, who have established their own household but have no children

* family – main shoppers and chief income earners, under 65, with one or more children in their household

* late – includes all adults whose children have left home or who are over 35 and childless.

Occupation groups are defined as white or blue:

* white – chief income earner is in the ABC1 occupation group (see Social Grade).

* blue – chief income earner is in the C2DE occupation group (see Social Grade).

Sector Classification for the National Accounts

The Sector Classification for the National Accounts in the UK is consistent with the European System of Integrated Economic Accounts (ESA). Economic units – organisations and individuals – are classified into groups with similar characteristics so that their economic and financial behaviour can be aggregated for analysis.

SERVCOM

SERVCOM is an initiative, still in the early stages, to develop a classification scheme for service sectors and services similar to the existing PRODCOM classification (see that entry). See also Computer Services Survey in chapter 6.

Social Grade

Social grade classifications have been developed to categorise the population into social grades or strata. The most commonly used social grade classification in the UK was developed by Research Surveys Ltd for the Institute of Practitioners in Advertising in 1962 and is still used in major surveys such as the National Readership Survey (NRS) and Target Group Index (TGI). This classification has the following breakdowns:

A   upper middle class (managerial, professional)

B   middle class (administrative, professional)

C1   lower middle class (supervisory, clerical)

C2   skilled working class (skilled manual workers)

D   working class (semi-skilled and unskilled)

E   state pensioners, casual workers.

See other entries, including ESOMAR Social Grade Classification and National Statistics Socio-Economic Classification.

Socio-economic Classification

Socio-economic classifications are classifications which ascertain social and economic characteristics of a given population and may be based on a number of criteria. For example, labour force status, occupation etc. See National Statistics Socio-Economic Classification.

Standard Classification of Products by Activity in the European Economic Community

The Standard Classification of Products by Activity in the European Economic Community (CPA) is the European version of the Central Product Classification (see that entry) developed by the United Nations. However, unlike the CPC, the CPA is legally binding on member states. The CPA is broken down into six levels:

Level 1 17 sectors broken down into another 31 sub-sectors

Level 2 60 divisions identified by a two-digit code

Level 3 221 groups identified by a three-digit code

Level 4 490 classes identified by a four-digit code

Level 5 947 categories identified by a five-digit code

Level 6 2,303 sub-categories identified by a six-digit code.

Standard Industrial Classification

The Standard Industrial Classification (SIC) is the classification used in the UK to classify economic activity. Published official statistics on economic activities in the UK are usually based on the SIC. Most countries have a similar classification of economic activities although there is little harmonisation between these classifications: each country has developed its own classification based on its own economic structure. The UK SIC should not be confused with the US SIC, which is a separate classification. First introduced in the UK in 1948, the SIC has been revised at various times since as the business structure of the UK economy has changed. Revised classifications have been produced in 1958, 1968, 1980, and 1992.

The UK SIC is a hierarchical system of division of economic activities including manufacturing; construction; utilities; agriculture, forestry, and fisheries; and services.

The classification codes are a mixture of letters and numbers arranged in sections, subsections, divisions, groups, classes, and subclasses.

Sections – 17 sections covering major economic activities, e.g. manufacturing, agriculture, health, and social work. Each section is identified by a single letter as follows:

A   Agriculture, hunting and forestry

B   Fishing

C   Mining and quarrying

D   Manufacturing

E   Electricity, gas & water supply

F   Construction

G   Wholesale and retail trade; repair of motor vehicles, motoring and personal and household goods

H   Hotels and restaurants

I   Transport, storage and communications

J   Financial intermediaries

K   Real estate, renting and business activities

L   Public administration and defence, compulsory social security

M   Education

N   Health and social welfare

O   Other community, social and personal services activities

P   Private households with employed persons

Q   Extra-territorial bodies and organisations

Subsections – some larger sections are divided into sub-sections, e.g. AB, AC, etc.

Divisions – two-digit breakdown of sections and sub-sections, e.g. 17, 18, 19, etc.

Groups – divisions are broken down into groups identified by three digits, e.g. 17.4

Classes – groups are broken down into classes identified by four digits, e.g. 17.40

Subclasses – some classes are broken down into subclasses, e.g. 17.40/1

Here is one example of the above hierarchical system in the manufacturing section:

Section D   Manufacturing

Subsection DM   Manufacture of Transport Equipment

Division 35   Manufacture of Other Transport Equipment

Group 35.4   Manufacture of Motorcycles and Bicycles

Class 35.42   Manufacture of Bicycles

For other industrial classifications, see Industrial Classifications.

Standard International Trade Classification

Not to be confused with the SIC described above, the Standard International Trade Classification (SITC) is a classification of international trade produced by the United Nations. It is the longest established international trade classification and its latest revision took place in 1988. Although still used by many countries when compiling their official international trade and product import/export data, it has been replaced as the main classification used in most countries by the more detailed Harmonised Commodity Description and Coding System (see that entry).

The classification has sections and divisions covering sectors and main product groups within these sectors and it is further subdivided into individual product headings with a four- or five-digit code. For example:

Section 8   Miscellaneous manufactured articles

Division 88   Photographic apparatus, equipment & supplies; optical goods; watches and clocks

881.21   Cinematographic cameras

Standard Occupational Classification

The Standard Occupational Classification (SOC) is the classification used to provide an occupational breakdown which forms the basis for the compilation of UK official statistics on the labour market. The SOC was introduced in 1990 and the classification was revised in 2000 to incorporate industrial and occupational changes. SOC2000 was used alongside SOC90 (the original classification) in the Summer 2000 Labour Force Survey (LFS). The main features of the revision of the classification include a tighter definition of managerial occupations and an overhaul of new occupations introduced as a result of new technology.

In the classification, jobs are classified according to their skill level and content and the classification is segmented in major groups, sub-major groups, minor groups, and unit groups. For example:

Major Group I   Managers and senior officials

Sub-Major Groups II   Corporate managers

Minor Group III   Corporate managers and senior officials

Unit Group IIII   Senior officials in national government

In 1992, the European Union began the process of harmonisation of occupational classification schemes used in individual member countries.

Standard Statistical Regions

Standard Statistical Regions (SSRs) are South West, South East, East Anglia, Wales, West Midlands, East Midlands, North West, Yorkshire & Humberside, North, Scotland, and Northern Ireland. Other regional classifications include Government Office Regions, NHS regional office areas, Environment Agency regions, and Tourist Board regions (see these entries).

Sub-Saharan Africa

In international statistical publications, the geographical region described as Sub-Saharan Africa usually covers all of Africa excluding Algeria, Egypt, Libyan Arab Jamahiriya, Morocco, Tunisia, Nigeria, and South Africa.

System of National Accounts

The System of National Accounts (SNA) was devised by the United Nations to give common definitions for national accounts data, input-output tables, and financial accounts. The latest version was published in 1993. National accounts statistical series from the United Nations are based on the SNA.

Tourist Board Regions

Tourist Board regions in the UK are West Country, Southern, South East England, London, East of England, Heart of England, Wales, North West, Yorkshire, Cumbria, Northumbria, Scotland, and Northern Ireland. Other regional classifications include Government Office Regions, Standard Statistical Regions, NHS regional office areas, and Environment Agency regions (see those entries).

UK Sector Classification Guide for the National Accounts

The UK Sector Classification Guide for the National Accounts is a classification of businesses, charities, and other public and private organisations for compilation of the National Accounts. It is updated every few years by National Statistics.

UNCTAD Classification of Economies

In some of its statistical publications, the United Nations Conference on Trade and Development (UNCTAD) (see also chapter 6) uses a classification of economies to place countries into specific income categories. In its 2000 publications, the classification for low income, middle income, and high income areas is as follows:

low income   countries with a 1995 per capita GDP of less than US$800

middle income   countries with a 1995 per capita GDP of more than US$800 but less than US$4,000

high income   countries with a 1995 per capita GDP of more than US$4,000

See also Classifications of Economies and World Bank Classification of Economies.

United Nations Economic Commission for Europe

The United Nations Economic Commission for Europe (UN/ECE) (see also Chapter 6) consists of all the countries of Western Europe, Eastern Europe and the territory of the former Soviet Union, North America, and Israel.

Western Asia

In international statistical publications, the geographical area of Western Asia usually refers to Bahrain, Cyprus, Iran, Iraq, Israel, Jordan, Kuwait, Lebanon, Oman, Quatar, Saudi Arabia, Syrian Arab Republic, Turkey, United Arab Emirates, and Yemen.

World Bank Classification of Economies

For its core statistical publications and series, the World Bank's main criteria for classifying economies is gross national product (GNP) per capita. Every economy is classified as low income, middle income (subdivided into lower middle and upper middle) or high income. The income groups are based on GNP per capita for the latest year available but GNP per capita can change over time so the country composition of income groups may change from one year to the next. For the year 2000, the income groups are:

low-income economies   GNP per capita of US$760 or less in 1998.

middle-income economies   GNP per capita of more than US$760 but less than US$9,360. Lower middle-income and upper middle-income economies are separated at a GNP per capita of $3,030.

high-income economies   GNP per capita of US$9,361 or more. The participating member countries of the European Monetary Union (EMU) are presented as a sub-group under high-income economies.

See also Classifications of Economies and UNCTAD Classification of Economies.

2

Economic and financial statistics

Published statistics are dominated by economic and financial statistics, with most of these published by central governments or central government agencies. Other publishers include central banks and other financial institutions, stock exchanges, stockbrokers and financial analysts, and economic research and forecasting organisations. The publication of economic and financial data can have a major impact on government policy, consumer and business expectations and confidence, and national and world financial markets. In the short term, a poor set of published economic data can wipe billions off the value of shares. In the longer term, these statistics offer a picture of trends in a specific economy or a group of economies, and support the detailed analysis of these trends.

Economic indicators such as gross domestic product (GDP), retail prices, exchange rates, balance of payments, personal disposable income, and unemployment rates are regularly quoted and discussed in the press and media. This chapter explains these core indicators found in economic and financial statistical publications with particular reference to UK economic and financial indicators.

Probably the most important economic indicator is GDP, as it is a measure of the size of a specific economy, the growth or otherwise in a specific economy, and the structure of a specific economy. Aggregated and disaggregated GDP data forms the basis of the national accounts of most countries but it can be a confusing indicator as it is measured in various ways. These are described in this chapter.

Prices are another important component of economic analysis as price changes have a major impact on the economic well-being of all economic players – consumers, companies, governments, and others. Again, price statistics can be confusing as there are numerous price series measuring prices in different sectors and for different economic groups. There have also been some new price measures introduced recently to offer a more comprehensive picture of prices across all sectors of the economy. This chapter describes the various indices including traditional series such as the Retail Price Index (RPI), Producer Price Index (PPI), and Wholesale Price Index (WPI). There are new series such as the Final Expenditure Price Index (FEPI), introduced recently to offer a more comprehensive view of the overall economy, the Corporate Services Price Index (CSPI), designed to monitor prices in the service sector, and the Harmonised Indices of Consumer Prices (HICP) offering comparable price data across the European Union. Mention should also be made of the GDP Deflator (or Implicit Price Deflator), a measure of price change derived from GDP data.

Economic and financial indicators

Activity Rate

Used in labour market analysis, the activity rate expresses the labour force as a percentage of the population of working age.

Australian Share Indices

Share price indices on the Australian Stock Exchange are led by the ASX All Ordinaries Index (covering shares of 300 of the most actively traded companies) and ASX 100 Index (top 100 companies).

Average Earnings Index

The Average Earnings Index (AEI) is designed to measure changes in the level of earnings, i.e. wage inflation. Average earnings are calculated as the total wages and salaries paid by firms, divided by the number of employees paid. The AEI is based on the monthly Wages and Salary Survey covering a sample of firms in Great Britain. The sample covers the wage bill for some 9 million employees, and the AEI is published monthly. The main indicator of growth, the headline rate, is based on the annual change in the seasonally adjusted index value for the latest three months compared with the same period a year ago. The use of a three-month average reduces the level of volatility seen in the data each month. There is an AEI for the whole economy and specific AEIs for private sector, public sector, manufacturing, production, and services. The sample survey on which the AEI is based is not completely representative of the economy as firms with fewer than 20 employees are excluded, as are the earnings of the self-employed. The AEI is published monthly in the *Labour Market Statistics First Release* and other sources are *Economic Trends* and *Labour Market Trends*.

Balance of Payments

The Balance of Payments (BOP) is a record of all transactions during a specific period between residents of a country or economic area and the rest of the world. The BOP must balance: it is built up on the basis of double-entry book keeping.

There are two main accounts in the BOP:

- Current Account – records imports and exports of goods and services
- Capital Account – measures flow of funds across national borders.

As the BOP must balance, a deficit or surplus on one account must be matched by an equal and opposite deficit or surplus on the other account. However, in the practical calculations of BOP, there is usually a 'black hole' due to the problem of recording invisibles accurately (see Balance of Payments – Current Account) and financial investment flows (see Balance of Payments – Capital Account).

Detailed annual balance of payments figures are published in the *UK Balance of Payments – the Pink Book* (see that entry in chapter 6) and provisional quarterly figures are published in *First Releases*. A relatively recent initiative has been the compilation of data covering international trade in services (see International Trade in Services Survey and *UK Trade in Services* in chapter 6).

Balance of Payments – Capital Account
The BOP – Capital Account records long-term capital flows and short-term capital flows between countries and economic areas, as well as changes in a country's gold and convertible currency reserves. An example of a long-term capital flow would be investment in buildings, plant, or machinery by a foreign company in a specific economy. Short-term capital flows include speculative investments in foreign exchange or short-term assets, plus official flows of currency, gold, etc.

Balance of Payments – Current Account
The BOP – Current Account records imports and exports of goods and services. It is divided into two separate accounts known as the 'Visible Balance' and the 'Invisible Balance'. The Visible Balance, often referred to as the Balance of Trade, records the imports and exports of physical goods such as food, electronic equipment, vehicles, textiles, and clothing, etc. The Invisible Balance records imports and exports of services, such as financial services, consultancy, and tourism, etc., and also includes income from interest, profits, and dividends, plus transfers (such as residents of one country sending money to another country).

The Visible Balance is easier to calculate as it is dealing with physical goods, and quantities and values of these goods can be measured relatively easily.

Balance of Trade

The Balance of Trade does not cover the total account of the Balance of Payments but refers to the Visible Balance of Trade (see entry above). The Visible Balance records the imports and exports of physical goods.

Canadian Share Indices

Share price indices for the Toronto Stock Exchange (TSE) include the TSE 300 Composite Index and TSE 100 Index.

Composite Leading Indicators

Composite Leading Indicators (CLIs) are designed to predict cyclical changes (peaks and troughs) in aggregate economic activity. They normally comprise a set of component series chosen from key economic indicators. For example, these components might be industrial production, order books, unemployment, or share prices, etc. Examples can be found in the monthly OECD publication *Main Economic Indicators*. For further information see Cyclical Indicators in chapter 7.

Consumer Confidence Indicator

Consumer confidence measures consider the perceptions amongst consumers of their economic well-being. Generally, the more optimistic consumers are about their economic situation, and their economic position in the next three, six, or 12 months, then the more likely they are to spend money on goods and services. Consumer confidence survey results can be used as a leading indicator (see Cyclical Indicators in chapter 7) to help predict short term changes in the economy.

The Consumer Confidence Indicator is the arithmetic average of the answers (balances) to four questions on the financial situation of households, general economic situation, and major purchases asked in the Consumer Survey carried out in EU member countries (see Opinion Polls and Business Surveys in chapter 5).

Consumer's Expenditure

See Household Final Consumption Expenditure.

Corporate Services Price Index

The Corporate Services Price Index (CSPI) is a new index tracking prices in the corporate services sector. Sectors such as business and professional services, telecommunications, and road freight are covered. Excluded are any services provided to final consumers which are included in the Retail Price Index (RPI). The monthly index fills a gap in the measurement of inflation in the UK and will complement the RPI and Producer Price Index (PPI).

Country Risk Ratings

Risk ratings are produced for most countries to allow investors and potential investors in these countries to assess the political, economic, and financial risks associated with the countries concerned. Separate risk ratings can be produced for political, economic, business, and financial prospects, or all these may be combined in a single risk assessment rating. Risk ratings are usually based on various components which are then converted into a single risk assessment rating. Most risk ratings are either numerical or alphabetical indexes. For example, the risk ratings produced by Political Risk Service Group (PRS) include separate ratings for political situation (PR – political rating), financial situation (FR – financial rating), and economic situation (ER – economic rating), and all three are combined in the Composite Risk Rating (CRR). The CRR includes information on 22 components of risk and this is converted into a single numerical risk assessment rating ranging from 0 to 100: ratings below 50 are considered very high risk, and those above 80 are considered very low risk. The ratings are updated every month. When alphabetical codes are used for risk ratings, a letter closer to the beginning of the alphabet means lower risk.

Some other producers of risk ratings include Euromoney Publications, Dun & Bradstreet, Standard & Poors, and Moody's.

Disposable Income

See National Disposable Income and Personal Disposable Income.

Dow Jones Indices

See New York Stock Exchange Indices.

Earnings

Published earnings data usually refers to the total gross remuneration employees receive before any statutory deductions, such as tax and national insurance.

Economic Sentiment Indicator

The Economic Sentiment Indicator is a composite measure used in business and consumer opinion surveys (see Opinion Polls and Business Surveys in chapter 5) in EU countries. The Industrial Confidence Indicator (in chapter 4), the Consumer Confidence Indicator (see above), and the Construction Confidence Indicator are combined with the share price index to produce the Economic Sentiment Indicator.

Economically Active

The economically active population are those who are either in employment or unemployed according to the International Labour Organisation (ILO) definition.

Economically Inactive

Economically inactive people are out of work but do not satisfy all the criteria for the International Labour Organisation (ILO) definition of unemployment, such as those in retirement and those who are not actively seeking work.

Employment

There are two main ways of measuring employment: the number of people in employment or the number of jobs. These two measures can produce different results as one person can have more than one job. In the Labour Force Survey (LFS), the main labour market survey, people aged 16 and over are classed as employed if they have done at least one hour of work in the reference week or are temporarily away from a job (e.g. on holiday). People are classified into one of four categories in the LFS according to their main job: employees, self-employed, unpaid family worker, participating in a government-supported training programme. In the UK, employment figures from the LFS in total and by sector are published quarterly. See *Labour Market Trends* (chapter 6).

The number of jobs is mainly collected through monthly postal employer surveys. These workplace surveys give the number of employee jobs (previously referred to as employees in employment). The total number of workforce jobs is calculated by summing employee jobs, self-employment jobs from the LFS, those in the armed forces, and government-supported trainees. In the UK, the number of jobs in total and by industry is published monthly. See *Labour Market Trends* (Chapter 6).

The LFS provides a more complete measure of employment than the workplace jobs surveys but the latter surveys probably provide a more accurate industrial breakdown than the LFS. Employment figures can be a guide to the overall performance of the economy and specific sectors. However, the split between full-time and part-time working is important. The number of hours worked is also important.

Employment Rate

The employment rate expresses persons in employment as a percentage of the population of working age.

Environmental Accounts

Environmental accounts are now an established component of the UK national accounts, and the national accounts of many other countries. These environmental accounts provide a link between environmental statistics and the profile of the economy given in standard national accounts. Environmental accounts try to show the extent to which the economy depends upon natural resources, and the impact of economic activity on the environment. They were first published in the UK in 1996 as pilot accounts for 1993. These accounts were updated and extended in 1998. In 1999 and 2000, environmental accounts have been included as summary accounts in *UK National Income – the Blue Book* (see that entry in chapter 6).

Environmental Indicators

Three international bodies – the OECD, the UN, and the World Bank – have agreed on six environmental indicators which should be monitored:

- countries with a national strategy for sustainable development
- population with access to safe water
- intensity of freshwater use
- nationally protected area as percentage of total land
- GDP per unit of energy use
- total and per capita carbon dioxide emissions.

See also Quality of Life Counts.

e-Tail Price Index

Established in July 2000, the e-Tail Price Index (e-TPI) monitors prices of 1,500 products and services sold on the Web. It is published monthly by financial services company Goldfish.

Exchange Rate

The exchange rate is the value of one currency expressed in another currency, e.g. the pound against the US dollar, the pound against the deutschmark, the yen against the franc, etc. The market rate is determined by market forces, i.e. the buying and selling of currency in the market. The official rate is determined by the monetary authorities.

In published statistical tables and other sources such as international market reports, value figures in one national currency may be converted to another currency. Very often, this is done to show market sizes and trends in each national market in a common currency such as the US dollar, pound, or Euro. In these currency conversions, fluctuations in exchange rates can have a significant effect on the data. For example, a negative trend shown in national currency values can turn into an upward trend when expressed in a common currency and vice versa. This is likely to reflect significant changes in the exchange rate rather than any major change in the national market.

Foreign exchange deals may be negotiated for settlement no more than two working days later, and these are referred to as spot deals. Foreign exchange deals settled at some future date are known as forward deals. Spot rates and forward rates are published rates and the rate for a forward deal is generally expressed by showing the amount by which the forward rate diverges from the spot rate, either in value terms or as a percentage.

The main exchange rates against the pound are published daily in many national newspapers. More detailed time series are published in *Financial Statistics* (see chapter 6).

Final Consumption Expenditure

Final consumption expenditure is expenditure on goods and services that are used for the direct satisfaction of individual needs or the collective needs of members of a community. This is distinct from the purchase of goods and services for use in the production process, which is referred to as intermediate consumption expenditure. See also Household Final Consumption Expenditure.

Final Expenditure Prices Index

In response to requests for a wider inflation measure than traditional price indices (see Producer Price's Index and Retail Price's Index), UK statisticians have developed the Final Expenditure Price's Index (FEPI). The transactions covered in the index are final purchases by UK residents, and these cover consumer expenditure, investment expenditure, and government expenditure. The new index covers the economy more widely than existing indices and it is being published experimentally in monthly issues of *Economic Trends*. There is a general FEPI and specific indices for consumer prices, investment prices, and government prices.

Fixed Capital Formation

Fixed Capital Formation is the usual terminology used in statistical time series to indicate investment in capital equipment, e.g. plant, buildings, and machinery. It includes the value of any services embodied in the fixed capital goods acquired. Fixed capital formation can be recorded as gross fixed capital formation (including consumption of fixed capital), or net fixed capital formation (excluding consumption of fixed capital).

French Share Indices

Leading indices of shares on the Paris Stock Exchange are the CAC 40 Index and SBF 250 Index. The former, launched in 1988, comprises 40 of the most representative French stock. The latter is the top 250 companies.

FT 30

The FT 30, previously known as FT Ordinary Share (30 Share) Index is published daily by the FT and also published in *Financial Statistics*. The constituents of the index are 30 market leaders representing a cross-section of British industry, although it is biased towards major industrial and retailing companies. Financial and oil stocks are now included. All shares in the index are unweighted so, over the long term, it has a downward bias. It is useful as a short-term indicator of the UK stock market.

FT Non-Financials Share Index

Originally the FT-500 Share Index, this was renamed the Non-Financials Share Index on 31 December 1993. It comprises five main sections: mineral extraction, general industrial, consumer goods, services, and utilities.

FTSE™ AIM Index

This gives share prices for young and growing companies listed on the Alternative Investment Market (AIM).

FTSE™ All-Share

The FTSE All-Share Index (name changed from FT-SE Actuaries All-Share Index) contains over 900 companies resident and domiciled in the UK. The prices used in the calculation of these indices are exact mid-prices taken at the close of business each day. The index is constantly monitored to reflect changes in the UK's economic structure. The index is published daily in the FT and monthly in *Financial Statistics*.

FTSE™ Eurotop 300

This is an index of the shares of the top 300 European companies.

FTSE™ techMARK™ All-Share

This index gives share prices in the market for innovative technology companies. The index was launched in November 1999.

FTSE™ techMARK™ 100

This index lists share prices for the top 100 innovative technology companies.

FTSE™ 100

The FTSE 100 was introduced in January 1984 in response to demands for a real-time index. The index is based on the 100 shares of the largest companies by market capitalisation. There are regular revisions to the companies included in the FTSE 100 and specific companies are removed when their market capitalisation falls too low. The index is published daily in the FT and monthly in *Financial Statistics*.

FTSE™ 250

The FTSE 250 is a real-time index of the next 250 companies in market capitalisation ranking below the FTSE 100. It was first published in 1992. The index is published daily in the FT and monthly in *Financial Statistics*.

FTSE™ 350

The FTSE 350 combines the FTSE 100 and the FTSE 250. It is published daily in the FT and monthly in *Financial Statistics*.

FTSE4Good

Launched in Summer 2001, the FTSE4Good is a new family of ethical indices developed in association with the Ethical Investment Research Service (EIRIS). FTSE4Good consists of four indices in total, covering the UK, US, Europe, and the world.

GDP

See Gross Domestic Product

German Share Indices

Leading indices of shares on the German Stock Exchange (Deutsche Borse AG) are CDAX German Corporate Index, and DAX 100 Index.

Gross Domestic Product

Gross Domestic Product (GDP) is arguably the most important economic indicator and it measures the size of an economy in three different ways:

- Expenditure – measures spending by economic agents on goods and services produced/supplied from a specific country or economic area.

- Income – measures income of residents of a specific country or economic area, whether individual or corporate, derived from the current production of goods and services.

- Output – measure of the value added created by each industry/ business sector in a specific country or economic area.

In economic theory, the three measures of GDP produce the same value figure for GDP but, in practice, the three measures often differ because of the different ways in which each indicator is calculated.

As well as measuring the size of an economy at a given time, GDP growth is used as an indicator of economic growth while measures of GDP per head or GDP per capita are used to compare national or regional affluence.

Gross Domestic Product – Expenditure Measure

The GDP – Expenditure Measure is one of the three main ways of measuring GDP. It measures the total paid by final purchasers for goods and services, either for final consumption or for capital goods. The largest component of the expenditure measure is consumer's expenditure (Household Final Consumption Expenditure) on goods and services and other components are government expenditure and capital goods spending, usually referred to as gross fixed capital formation (see Fixed Capital Formation). The value of exports of goods and services are also included as the expenditure on these goods and services is paid to domestic producers but the value of imports is subtracted from the calculation.

By analysing the various components of the GDP – Expenditure Measure, it is possible to track trends in consumer expenditure, investment, the size of the public sector in relation to the total economy, and a country's trade performance in relation to the whole economy.

Published quarterly as a provisional figure in *First Release: UK Output, Income and Expenditure*; published annually in detail in *UK National Accounts – Blue Book*. A useful source of international comparisons is *OECD National Accounts – Detailed Aggregates*.

Gross Domestic Product – Income Measure

The GDP – Income Measure is one of the three main ways of measuring GDP. It measures the income of residents of an economy and these can be individuals, corporate entities, or public corporations. Only income from productive activities is included and this is usually described as 'factor incomes', i.e. income from labour, land, and capital. The main components are income from employment, gross trading profits of companies, gross trading surplus of public corporations and government enterprises, and other income such as rents and income from self-employment. The calculation only includes 'domestic' income, i.e. income generated within a specific economy. Excluded is income generated by residents from activities outside the domestic economy (in foreign locations) – when this is added to 'domestic' income, the total is known as 'national' income and this is used to calculate another indicator, Gross National Product (GNP); see that entry. Excluded from the calculation of GDP – Income Measure are 'transfer payments' such as state benefits.

The GDP – Income Measure can be used to assess the level of profits available for investment in an economy, the level of, and changes in, consumer income, and for measuring the rate of return on businesses. See sources mentioned in previous entry for GDP – Income Data.

Gross Domestic Product – Local Areas
GDP figures are published for regions and other local areas in the UK and other European countries. Eurostat also publishes pan-European figures for the key regions in each EU member country. In the UK, GDP data is available at three sub-national levels corresponding to the Nomenclature of Territorial Units for Statistics (NUTS) classification (see that entry in chapter 1):

1   Government Office Regions, Scotland, Wales, Northern Ireland

2   37 areas, sometimes referred to as sub-regions

3   133 areas which are generally groups of unitary authorities or districts, and sometimes referred to as local areas

Gross Domestic Product – Output Measure
The GDP – Output Measure is one of the three main ways of measuring GDP. It measures the Value Added (see that entry) created by each industry and sector of the economy and aggregates each sector's figure to produce a total GDP – Output Measure figure for the whole economy. The measure includes the output of service industries as well as production industries and agriculture, construction, and utilities.

As well as producing a total figure for the whole economy, the GDP – Output Measure breaks down total GDP by industry and sector. This enables valued added figures for specific sectors to be obtained and it is a useful way to measure the importance of a specific sector in a particular economy and to measure growth in a specific sector compared with overall economic growth. Value added figures for specific sectors can be expressed as a percentage of total GDP to produce an estimate of the importance of that sector to the economy. Comparing these annual percentages over a series of years can show how the relative importance of a sector to the national economy has changed over time.

For example, here are some figures for value added in the hotels and restaurants sector in the UK and total value added for the UK economy:

Gross value added at current prices £ million

	1991	1996	1999
Hotels and Restaurants	14,368	20,471	25,015
% of total value added	2.7	3.1	3.2
Total value added – all industries	523,137	674,029	787,386

Source: United Kingdom National Accounts Blue Book, 2000

The figures show the growing importance of the hotels and restaurants industry in the economy with its share of total value added increasing from 2.7% in 1991 to 3.2% in 1999.

Detailed GDP – Output Measure results are published annually and the measure is published as a value figure, i.e. £ million in the UK. The relevant detailed annual tables for the UK can be found in the *UK National Accounts – the Blue Book* in the 'UK industrial analysis' section. A useful source of international comparisons is the annual *OECD National Accounts – Detailed Results*.

Gross Domestic Product – Market Prices/Current Prices
All the measures of GDP described above can be expressed in market prices (sometimes referred to as current prices or actual prices). This means that GDP is valued at the actual prices prevailing in the specific time period to which the GDP figure refers. Valuing GDP at these actual prices may not give a true picture of the economy, or changes over time in the economy. This is particularly true if the economy is facing inflationary or deflationary pressures. GDP value expressed in market prices or current prices will reflect inflationary or deflationary trends rather than real growth in underlying economic activity. See Gross Domestic Product (GDP) – Constant Prices, and the explanation of Current Prices and Constant Prices in chapter 7 for more information.

Gross Domestic Product – Constant Prices
All the three measures of GDP described above can be expressed in constant prices (sometimes referred to as GDP value at current prices in national currencies, 1997–1999 where GDP is valued at the prices prevailing in some selected Base Year – see Index Numbers in chapter 7). Over time, changes in GDP at market prices show changes in the monetary value of the components of GDP and, as these changes in value can reflect changes in both price and volume, it is difficult to ascertain how much of an increase in the series is due either to increased activity in the economy or to an increase in the price level. Valuing GDP, and GDP growth, at constant prices removes any inflationary element from the calculation and gives a true picture of real growth in economic activity. See Current Prices and Constant Prices in chapter 7 for more information.

Gross Domestic Product – Factor Cost Prices
Final prices in some economic sectors, and for some products and services, can be distorted by taxes or subsidies: sectors facing VAT charges, for example, or products such as petrol, alcohol, and tobacco which face heavy taxes and duties. Sectors such as agriculture obtain subsidies which affect final prices. GDP calculations based on market prices (current prices/actual prices) in these sectors, and other sectors

with taxes or subsidies, would not give a true picture of underlying economic activity unless these taxes and subsidies are excluded. GDP at Factor Cost Prices values GDP at final purchase prices, excluding taxes and subsidies.

Gross Domestic Product – Per Head/Per Capita
GDP per head, or per capita, gives the value of GDP per head of population in a specific economy. It is based on the calculation dividing the value of GDP in a specific time period by the number of residents in the population of the economy. It is useful when comparing the affluence, or economic well-being, of different economic areas, i.e. countries or regions. For example, Luxembourg is a small country and its total GDP is much smaller than countries such as Germany and the UK. However, Luxembourg is an affluent country when compared with Germany and the UK, as shown by GDP per capita figures:

GDP in total and per head in US$ dollars at current prices, 1999

	Total GDP	GDP per capita
	BnUS$	US$
Germany	1,934	23,600
Luxembourg	17.1	39,300
UK	1,324	22,300

Source: OECD

Total GDP in Luxembourg was only US$17.1 billion in 1999, compared with US$1,934 billion in Germany. However, GDP per head in Luxembourg in 1999 was US$39,300 compared with only US$23,600 in Germany.

Gross Domestic Product Deflator

The GDP deflator (sometimes referred to as the implicit price deflator) measures the average annual rate of price change. It is not a direct measurement of prices, i.e. it is not calculated from actual price change of goods or services, but is derived implicitly by dividing GDP figures at current prices by GDP figures at constant prices. The GDP deflator is usually expressed as an index figure with a specific year as the base year. This index is usually referred to as the Implicit Price Index.

Gross Expenditure on Research & Development

Gross Expenditure on Research & Development (GERD) is an indicator of the total amount spent on R&D in the UK.

Gross National Income

Gross National Income (GNI) is calculated by adding net entrepreneurial and property income, and labour income, from abroad (i.e. outside the domestic economy) to gross domestic product (GDP) income measure. In other words, GNI is the value of all income earned by UK residents whether this income is earned in the UK or abroad. The GNI has replaced the use of GNP in the UK national accounts.

Gross National Product

See Gross National Income for a definition. In the UK, Gross National Product (GNP) has been replaced by Gross National Income (GNI) in the national accounts. In other countries, GNP is still the preferred terminology.

Gross World Product

The Gross World Product (GWP) is a measure of the total world economy and usually expressed as a percentage annual growth figure. It is published in the United Nation's *World Economic and Social Survey* and calculated as a weighted average of individual country's GDP growth rates.

Hang Seng Index

The Hang Seng Index is the main index of shares traded on the Hong Kong Stock Exchange.

Harmonised Indices of Consumer Prices

The Harmonised Indices of Consumer Prices (HICP) are calculated in each member state of the European Union for the purpose of European comparisons, required by the Maastricht Treaty. From January 1999, the HICP has been used by the European Central Bank as the measure for the definition of price stability across the euro area. The methodology for the construction of the HICP is similar to that of the Retail Price's Index (see that entry), but there are some differences in the two indicators. For example, a number of RPI series relating to housing costs, such as mortgage interest payments and buildings insurance, are excluded from the HICP, while HICP covers air fares, boats, and caravans, which are not in the RPI. HICP covers expenditure by a broader population base than the RPI. There are other differences which means that the two published indices produce slightly different indicators.

Household Final Consumption Expenditure

Household final consumption expenditure is the direct spending of resident households of a country on goods and services. General data on household final consumption expenditure is found in *UK National Accounts* (annual) and a more detailed breakdown by commodity and service is published in the quarterly *Consumer Trends*.

Household Satellite Account

The Household Satellite Account is linked to the main national accounts of the UK and it measures and values unpaid household work. Household production included in the Household Satellite Account has five main functions: providing housing, providing nutrition, providing clothing, providing care and education, and voluntary work.

House Prices

Trends and changes in house prices are used to gauge inflationary pressures and the buoyancy of the economy. Generally, increasing house prices are a sign of a buoyant economy as more consumers have the confidence to purchase a new house, or move house. There are national statistics on house price changes plus data for regions and local authority areas. However, these published statistics on house prices are difficult to compare as they are based on different samples. All house sales are reported to the HM Land Registry and it publishes quarterly house price trends in the *Residential Property Price Report* (see chapter 6). However, the results are not weighted to account for different types and sizes of houses and it is difficult to compare these figures with regular price series from sources such as the Nationwide or Halifax, which use their own property portfolios to calculate house prices and changes.

Implicit Price Deflator/Implicit Price Index

See Gross Domestic Product Deflator.

Income

A general definition of income is a flow of resources over a period, in cash or in kind. This definition separates income from wealth, which is the ownership of assets valued at a specific point in time. See Wealth.

There are various measures of income used in published statistics and these include Gross National Income (GNI), National Disposable Income (NDI), and Personal Disposable Income (PDI). See these entries for further details.

In the UK, net individual income refers to the gross personal income of individuals less income tax and National Insurance contributions. Gross individual income includes earnings, income from self-employment, investments and occupational pensions/annuities, benefit income, and income from miscellaneous other sources. Gross disposable household income includes the sum of the gross individual income above for all relevant members of the household. Disposable household income includes all flows of income into the household, net of tax, National Insurance contributions, council tax, contributions to occupational schemes, maintenance and child support payments, and parental contributions to students living away from home. Disposable household income figures can also be published in two formats: one including housing costs, and one after housing costs have been deducted. Housing costs consist of rent, water rates, community charges, mortgage interest payments, structural insurance, ground rent, and service charges.

There are two main official income series regularly produced in the UK. The first series – *Households Below Average Income* (HBAI) – provides information on the distribution of income based on the Family Resources Survey (FRS). The publication *Households Below Average Income* provides estimates of patterns of personal disposable income in Great Britain, and of changes in income over time in the UK. From 1994/95 onwards, HBAI provides data for Great Britain only and surveys individuals. The publication aims to measure potential living standards as determined by disposable income and, although it concentrates on the lower part of income distribution, comparisons are made with the upper part where relevant.

The second series – Redistribution of Income (ROI) – shows how government intervention through the tax and benefit system affects the income of households, and it includes the effects of indirect taxes such as VAT as well as estimating the cash value of benefits in kind. ROI provides estimates for the UK and surveys households. The ROI is published in *Economic Trends*.

Input–Output Tables

Input–output tables display the flow of goods and services in the economy in matrix form. They illustrate the relationship between producers and consumers and the interdependence among the different industries. In the UK, input–output tables show the intermediate transactions for over 120 different industries and corresponding commodity groups (or product groups). Published *Input–Output Tables for the United Kingdom* are available approximately every five years.

Interest Rates

The main interest rate measure up to August 1981 was the minimum lending rate (MLR). The MLR was introduced on 13 October 1972 and represented the minimum rate at which the Bank of England, acting as lender of last resort, normally lent to members of the discount market. Following the cessation of the continuous posting of MLR, the base rates of the retail banks now fulfil this role. *The Bank of England Quarterly Bulletin* and the monthly *Financial Statistics* provide data under the heading 'Selected Retail Banks Interest Rates' and this is based on the rates of the four leading banks – Barclays, Lloyds TSB, HSBC, and NatWest. Other rates regularly published in the above sources include building society interest rates, basic rate mortgages, interest rates for instant access and deposit accounts, and finance house base rates.

Intermediate Consumption Expenditure

Intermediate consumption expenditure is expenditure on consumption goods and services for use in the production process. This is distinct from final consumption expenditure which is expenditure on goods and services that are used for the direct satisfaction of individual needs or the collective needs of members of a community.

Labour Costs

Labour costs are defined as the total costs borne by employers in order to employ workers. These costs include direct costs, which are primarily wages and salaries and other earnings, and indirect costs, which might include social security contributions, vocational training costs, and taxes. The unit labour cost refers to the total expenditure on labour per unit of output. This can be calculated by dividing total labour costs by GDP.

Unit labour costs are a core indicator of the cost efficiency of labour: if unit labour costs fall, the same output can be produced for less expenditure on labour.

Labour Force

The labour force includes everyone in the labour market, i.e. employed and unemployed people.

Money Supply

There is no single definition of money used in the UK but there are two main measures. M0 is the narrowest definition of money, consisting mainly of notes and coins in circulation outside the Bank of England, but including also bankers' operational deposits at the Bank of England. M4 comprises the above plus holdings by the M4 private sector (i.e. private sector outside the monetary financial institutions) of notes and coins, together with sterling deposits at monetary financial institutions. These two measures are found in the monthly *Financial Statistics*. Other measures such as M1, M3, M3C have not been published since June 1989.

Money supply measures are useful as indicators of short-term spending: M0 tends to indicate small change spending, M4 is a better indicator of expenditure in general.

Morgan Stanley Capital International Indices

Morgan Stanley Capital International (MSCI) indices were the first international benchmarks constructed to satisfy a demand for a comparison of stock market trends in different countries. The MSCI indices were first established in 1969, and emerging markets were added in 1988. MSCI now covers over 3,000 securities in 23 developed markets and over 1,600 securities in 28 emerging markets. Historically, indices from specific stock exchanges have not been comparable with each other due to differences in the representation of the local market, mathematical formulae, base dates, and methods of adjusting for capital changes. MSCI indices use the same criteria and method of calculation across all markets. There are various indices available including World Index, All Country Indices (for all markets in a specific region), and Emerging Market Indices.

Nasdaq Indices

The Nasdaq Stock Market in New York provides information on share trends for IT, technology, biotechnology, and financial services companies. Its main indices are the Nasdaq Composite Index, which measures the market value of all common stocks listed on the Nasdaq Stock Market; Nasdaq-100 Index; Nasdaq Financial-100 Index; and Nasdaq National Market Composite Index.

National Accounts

The national accounts represent the economic accounts of a country and the regular basis of the UK national accounts is the quarterly GDP calculations. The national accounts are based on three GDP measures – output, income, expenditure – and the detailed national accounts tables break the whole economy down into institutional sectors. These 'sector accounts' provide disaggregated data on non-financial corporations (public and private), financial corporations, central government, local government, households, non-profit institutions serving households (NPISH), and the rest of the world.

The main aggregate and summary accounts, plus a detailed sector breakdown, for the UK is given in the annual *UK National Accounts – the Blue Book*. The *Quarterly National Accounts First Release* gives basic summary and disaggregated national accounts data while there are also summary national accounts tables in *Economic Trends, Monthly Digest of Statistics*, and *Annual Abstract of Statistics*. A useful source for international comparisons is *OECD National Accounts – Detailed Results*, published annually.

National Disposable Income

National Disposable Income (NDI) is defined as national income less net transfers abroad. It is interpreted as the nation's command over its goods and services.

New York Stock Exchange Indices

The New York Stock Exchange (NYSE) publishes various indices and the main ones are: NYSE Composite Index comprising all common stocks listed on the exchange; Dow Jones Stock Averages, compiled daily from NYSE closing prices; Standard & Poor's Composite Index of 500 Stocks; and the New York Stock Exchange Utility Index, consisting of companies in telecommunications, electrical services, gas, and other utilities.

Nikkei Stock Average

The Nikkei Stock Average, or Nikkei 225, is a leading indicator of share price changes on the Tokyo Stock Exchange. Other indices include the Nikkei 500. See also Tokyo Stock Price Index (TOPIX).

Pensioner Prices Index

As the spending patterns of pensioners are often quite different from those of most other groups in the population, a separate price index – the Pensioner Prices Index – has been developed for this group. For example, housing is excluded from the pensioner index because many pensioner households are in receipt of rent rebates or housing benefit so that increases in housing costs are not passed on in full.

Personal Disposable Income

Personal disposable income (PDI) is the aggregate of all incomes accruing to persons resident in a specific country or area, after taking into account all transfers and taxes on income. It represents that which persons spend on goods or services, or choose to save. It is equal to consumer spending plus savings. PDI may be quoted at market prices, i.e. without allowing for inflation. Real personal disposable income (RPDI) is real income after adjusting for inflation. Statistics are published in *Financial Statistics*. See also Total Personal Income.

Poverty Line

The poverty line is the minimum level (usually expressed in national currency) at which an individual or household in a specific economy can subsist. Measuring poverty can be problematic; issues include the differences between rural and urban poverty levels, or between different regions, within countries. The cost of living is typically higher in urban than in rural areas, so the urban poverty line should be higher than the rural one. However, not all cost of living indicators are higher in urban areas: public transport costs, for example, may be higher in rural areas. Differences in the circumstances of specific individuals and households also come into play. For example, individuals with regular access only to small, independent grocery shops may have to pay more for food compared with those able to use supermarkets regularly.

There are also international poverty measures based on international poverty lines, but international comparisons of poverty are even more problematic. In many highly developed countries, definitions of poverty based on amounts needed to maintain a minimum subsistence level are less applicable than they are in less developed countries. The current international poverty line, calculated using purchasing power parities (PPPs) and used in World Bank reports, is $1.08 a day.

See also Income.

Poverty Rate

The poverty rate is the percentage of the population living below the poverty line (see Poverty Line).

Producer Prices Index

The Producer Prices Index (PPI) measures the change, usually from month to month, in the output prices of manufacturing and production industries, and the input prices of materials and fuel purchased by business and industry. The input prices include prices of imported materials. The PPI is based on approximately 12,000 items collected from around 5,000 contributing companies. The PPI is a useful guide to industrial goods prices but it does not cover the service sector.

The PPI was published for the first time in August 1983, replacing the former Wholesale Price Index (WPI). The PPI is often seen as a useful guide to likely trends in retail inflation, as many price changes at the producer level are likely to be passed on to the retail sector. However, price changes in the PPI may not match future price changes in the retail price index (RPI) due to variations in manufacturer, wholesaler, retailer margins, or price discounting by retailers.

Most other countries have their own PPI, although some have a WPI. See Wholesale Price Index.

Productivity

Productivity is defined as the number of units of output (in the UK, measured by the Index of Production for the manufacturing sector and by GDP for the whole economy) produced by each filled job.

Public Expenditure and Revenues

Public expenditure is spending by government; revenues are government receipts, mainly from taxes and duties. Published statistics for this spending and revenues are produced monthly and annually. The percentage of GDP taken by public expenditure is a measure of the importance of the public sector in a specific economy. Public expenditure may be classified in various ways:

- by level of government, such as central government, local authorities, or government agencies
- by department, such as Ministry of Defence, Department of the Environment Food & Rural Affairs, or Home Office

- by function, such as IT services or environmental services, which might cut across various departments
- by economic category, such as current expenditure and capital expenditure.

Current expenditure includes spending on salaries and wages, goods and services, social security payments, and interest on the national debt. Capital expenditure mainly includes spending on fixed investment, infrastructure and buildings.

Government revenues are mainly raised though taxes, social security contributions, fees or charges for services, and some miscellaneous services such as interest on government loans.

The net total of government expenditure less revenues is the gap which has to be financed by borrowing, or which allows debt to be repaid. If there is a gap to be financed by borrowing, this is known as the Public Sector Borrowing Requirement (PSBR). A surplus allowing for debt re-payment is the Public Sector Debt Repayment (PSDR).

Statistics for government expenditure and revenues can be found in the detailed national accounts tables and publications described in chapter 6.

Purchasing Power of the Pound

Changes in the internal purchasing power of a currency may be de-fined as the opposite of changes in the levels of prices. When prices increase, the amount that can be purchased with a given sum of money falls. Conversely, when prices fall, the amount that can be purchased with a given sum of money increases. The Purchasing Power of the Pound indicator is created by taking the purchasing power as 100p in a specific time period (year, month, or quarter) and then calculating the comparable purchasing power in a subsequent year, month, or quarter based on inflation or deflation.

Purchasing Power Parities

In the comparison of value figures between countries, for example the value of production of a specific product, data converted at market exchange rates between the two countries may not give a true com-parison of the different countries' price levels. Figures expressed in purchasing power parities (PPPs) take into account these price differ-ences and give a truer comparison of values across countries. Many Eurostat and OECD publications include tables using PPPs.

Purchasing Power Standards – Conversion Rates Specific to Household Consumption

These PPS conversion rates indicate the national currency units needed, in the various countries, to purchase the same basket of goods and services.

Quality of Life Counts

As part of the UK government's sustainable development strategy, quality of life counts (QOLCs) have been created to provide indicators of progress. There are 147 indicators, and a sub-set of key headline indicators which focus on what sustainable development means and give a broad overview of what has been achieved. The key headline indicators are:

Economic progress

- GDP and GDP per head
- total investment and social investment as a percentage of GDP
- proportion of people of working age who are in work

Social progress

- indicators of success in tackling poverty and social exclusion
- qualifications at age 19
- expected years of healthy life
- homes judged as unfit to live in
- level of crime

Effective protection of the environment

- emissions of greenhouse gases
- days when air pollution is moderate or higher
- road traffic
- rivers of good or fair quality
- populations of wild birds
- new homes built on previously developed land

Prudent use of natural resources

- waste arising and management.

Further details can be found on the Web site of the Department of Environment, Food and Rural Affairs (DEFRA): *www.defra.org.uk.*

Quality of Life Indicators

Gross Domestic Product (GDP), the traditional measure of economic growth and well-being, fails to take into account other indicators of a nation's well-being such as environmental and social developments. Quality of life indicators have been developed to offer a measure of social, cultural and environmental trends and can cover a range of variables. The World Bank, for example, uses the following quality of life indicators in its publication *World Development Indicators*: pollution, sanitation, life expectancy at birth, levels of child malnutrition, and adult illiteracy rate. In the UK, there are quality of life counts (see that entry) which have been developed as part of the government's sustainable development strategy. Specific environmental indicators and environmental accounts (see those entries) have also been created to provide other indicators alongside the traditional economic measures.

Retail Prices Index

A retail prices index (RPI) measures the change, usually from month to month, in the average level of prices of goods and services purchased by households. In the UK, the RPI covers 600 separate goods and services for which price movements are regularly measured in 146 locations throughout the country. The basket of 600 goods and services is reviewed each year. The expenditure pattern on which the index is based is revised each year using information from the Family Expenditure Survey (see that entry in chapter 6) and the expenditure of certain higher income households and households of retired people dependent mainly on social security benefits is excluded. The RPI is the main indicator of consumer price inflation and it excludes industrial and business-to-business goods and services. It also contains some highly variable components which can result in sharp monthly swings in inflation, e.g. seasonal foods, mortgage interest payments, and indirect taxes.

A general RPI is published every month along with RPIs for specific products and services. There are also variations on the basic RPI published: RPIX covers all items except mortgage interest payments; RPIY covers all items except mortgage interest payments and indirect taxes.

Changes in prices for specific products and sectors can be monitored over time and compared with changes in the general RPI. The RPI is published in index form using an earlier year as the base year (e.g. 1995 = 100). The consumer inflation rate is usually expressed as a percentage change in one period compared with an earlier period, and this percentage change is calculated from the RPI.

Savings and Savings Ratio

National savings are defined as the total savings in the economy. These total savings include savings by the private sector (persons and companies) and government savings (government revenue less government expenditure). The national savings ratio is savings as a percentage of GDP.

Personal savings are calculated from Personal Disposable Income (see that entry) less personal consumption (i.e. spending on goods and services). Sometimes, data is also produced for household savings which equates to household disposable income less household expenditure. The savings ratio is savings as a percentage of disposable income. Savings ratios data can be found in, or calculated from, detailed national accounts publications.

SDR

The SDR is the unit of account used by the International Monetary Fund (IMF) and national currency values are converted to SDRs in some IMF statistical tables, for example, some indicators in the IMF's monthly publication *International Financial Statistics*. The value of the SDR is determined daily by the IMF on the basis of a basket of currencies with each currency assigned a weight. Since 1981, the value of the SDR has been determined on the basis of the currencies of the five member countries having the largest exports of goods and services in the five-year period before the date of the latest revision of the basket.

Share Price Index

The share price index is usually an index of common shares of companies trading on national or foreign stock exchanges. Share price indexes are typically produced daily, weekly, and monthly and are based on an aggregation of share prices and their movements in a specific time period. Some share price indexes only cover the top companies trading, or companies in a specific sector such as IT, while others cover all companies. See various entries for specific share indices, for example FT 30 (London Stock Exchange), New York Stock Exchange Indices, and Nasdaq Indices.

Shop Price Index

The Shop Price Index (SPI) is published monthly by the British Retail Consortium (BRC) and monitors trends in prices of 200 commonly purchased goods in UK retail outlets.

Solomon Smith Barney Global Equity Indices

The Solomon Smith Barney Global Equity Indices (SS-BGEI) are a series of indices covering all levels of market capitalisation across 49 countries.

Standard & Poor's Indices

Standard & Poor's publishes various share price and other indices for US, European and global equities. The major ones are:

- S&P 500
- S&P Global 1200
- S&P Europe
- S&P Mid Cap 400
- S&P Small Cap 600
- S&P Super Composite 1500
- S&P 100
- S&P REIT Index.

See also New York Stock Exchange Indices.

Sterling Effective Exchange Rate Index

The Sterling Effective Exchange Rate Index (ERI) shows the trends in the sterling exchange rate against a basket of 20 currencies. It is expressed as an index with the current base year at 1990. See *Financial Statistics* and *Economic Trends* in chapter 6).

Stock Market Trends

Stock market trends and changes are closely related to an economy's overall development. Share prices are a regular indicator of stock market performance, and details of some of the leading specific share price indices are given in relevant entries in this chapter. There are also measures of stock market size such as market capitalisation, turnover ratio, and the number of listed domestic companies.

Market capitalisation, sometimes referred to as market value, is calculated by multiplying share price by the number of shares outstanding. The turnover ratio is the value of shares traded as a percentage of market capitalisation. Another indicator is market liquidity, the ability to easily buy and sell securities. This is measured by dividing the total value traded by gross domestic product (GDP).

Tax and Price Index

The Tax and Price Index (TPI) was devised as a single index to measure changes in both direct taxes (including National Insurance contributions) and in retail prices for a cross-section of taxpayers in the UK. The TPI measures the change in gross taxable income needed for taxpayers to maintain their purchasing power allowing for changes in retail prices. While the Retail Price Index (RPI) just measures changes in prices, the TPI considers tax changes on consumers as well as price changes.

Terms of Trade

The terms of trade measure the relative prices of a country's exports and imports. The common method of calculating the terms of trade is the net barter, or commodity, terms of trade. This is the ratio of the export price index to the import price index. When the net barter terms of trade increases, a country's exports are becoming more valuable or its imports cheaper. When the net barter terms of trade decreases, a country's exports are becoming cheaper or its imports are becoming more valuable.

Tokyo Stock Price Index

The Tokyo Stock Price Index (TOPIX) is a composite index of all common shares listed on the first section of the Tokyo Stock Exchange. It is supplemented by sub-indices for each of 33 industry groups. There are various other TOPIX indices including the TOPIX Core 30, TOPIX100, and TOPIX500. See also Nikkei Stock Average.

Total Personal Income

Total personal income is the aggregate of incomes accruing from work or property and from social security and other benefits. In the UK, Personal disposable income (see that entry) is obtained by deducting UK taxes on income, national insurance, etc. and transfers abroad from total personal income.

Unemployment

There are currently two main measures of unemployment in the UK. The traditional measure is based on the numbers claiming unemployment-related benefit at benefit offices. This measure is based on an administrative procedure – the benefit system – and it has been criticised in recent years as more people have been ineligible to claim benefits. It is published monthly with detailed figures in *Labour Market Trends*.

A second measure of unemployment is collected from the Labour Force Survey (see that entry in chapter 6) and is based on the International Labour Organisation (ILO) definition of unemployment: people without a job who were available to start work in two weeks following their Labour Force Survey interview, and had looked for work in the four weeks prior to interview.

Both measures give the number of persons unemployed and the unemployment rate. The latter is the unemployed as a percentage of people in the labour force. The LFS provides a more complete measure of unemployment than the claimant count, especially for women, and is better suited to international comparisons (most European countries have an LFS using the ILO definitions). OECD publishes standardised unemployment rates for its member countries based on the ILO definition. The claimant count is more useful in assessing unemployment in small areas (below the level of regions).

Unemployment can be used as a measure of economic performance, i.e. high unemployment suggests a weaker economy, high unemployment may significantly weaken any positive effects of growth in GDP. In the latter scenario, total GDP may be growing but GDP per head for many members of the population may not be growing, and may be falling, if they are unemployed and unable to reap the benefits of GDP growth. See *Labour Market Trends* (chapter 6) for the regular data.

Value Added

The value generated by any unit engaged in production, and the contribution of individual sectors or industries to GDP. Value added is used instead of the value of output of specific sectors for the GDP calculation because using the latter indicator would lead to double counting. For example, the motor vehicle industry buys steel and plastic from other industries and these materials are used in the manufacture of finished vehicles. If the value of the output of the motor vehicles industry was used in the GDP calculation the value of the steel and plastics output would be counted twice – once when calculating the value of output of the steel and plastics industries and again when calculating the value of output of the motor vehicles sector. The value added calculation excludes the value of any materials, goods, or services bought from another sector. GDP data by industry and sector is often published under the heading 'Value Added by Industry'. The *UK National Accounts – the Blue Book* has a value added by industry table.

Wealth

Published statistics on personal wealth in the UK usually refer to marketable wealth of all adults in the UK. Wealth is defined as the ownership of assets valued at a specific point in time. This wealth can be divided into marketable and non-marketable. Marketable wealth can be sold, but non-marketable wealth is usually tied up in pension schemes or other financial arrangements and cannot be sold. Data on the distribution of wealth is produced by the Inland Revenue.

Wholesale Price Index

The Wholesale Price Index (WPI) measures price changes for agricultural and industrial goods at various stages of production. In the UK, the WPI has largely been replaced by the Producer Price's Index (see that entry) which is more easily incorporated into national accounts calculations. Some countries, such as Austria and Greece, still produce a WPI, and others produce both WPI and PPI figures. These latter countries include Denmark, Germany, Ireland, and Japan.

3

Demographic Statistics

Indicators of population size, change, and characteristics are important for local and central government planning and policies. They are also used by a range of businesses for marketing and market research, and by many other organisations. Demographic data may also be used to balance and interpret economic data: for example, total GDP in a country may be rising year-on-year but, if the annual population increase in that country is even stronger, then GDP per capita is likely to be weakening.

The most important source of population data in the UK, as in many other countries, is the population census which is currently undertaken every 10 years. The census is almost a complete count of the total population: census questionnaires are delivered or sent to every household and communal establishment and the response rate is close to 100%. The results are analysed not only at national level but for regions, counties, local authority areas, and even smaller areas, and the ability to provide data at both national and very local level makes the population census unique. All developed countries undertake regular censuses, and harmonisation of national censuses across the European Union is now under way.

In some countries, such as the Netherlands, where a national population register is updated at very regular intervals and residents are obliged to update their records on these registers if they move, the census is less important as a count of the population but does provide other information on demographic and household characteristics.

In between the census years, there are numerous other population series offering data at national, sub-national and local level and these are led by annual population estimates, population projections, and statistics on specific demographic themes and issues such as births, deaths, marriages, divorces, migration, and abortion.

Demographic indicators and definitions

Age Bands

Age breakdowns of demographic data are often presented in age bands, although the age bands used can vary from source to source. The data is often presented in five-year age bands but there may still be differences in the age ranges covered. For example, *Population Trends* in the UK has five-year age breakdowns up to the age of 89 but the *UN Demographic Yearbook* has five-year age breakdowns up to 84:

Sample age bands

Population Trends	UN Demographic Yearbook
under 1	under 1
1–4	1–4
5–9	5–9
10–14	10–14
15–19	15–19
20–24	20–24
25–29	25–29
30–34	30–34
35–39	35–39
40–44	40–44
45–49	45–49
50–54	50–54
55–59	55–59
60–64	60–64
65–69	65–69
70–74	70–74
75–79	75–79
80–84	80–84
85–89	85 and over
90 and over	

Most national population estimates and census data have data for single ages, although all this data may not be published: presenting the data in age bands is often an easier option. However, the annual *Mid-200- Population Estimates for England and Wales*, for example, has estimates broken down by single ages.

More specific surveys may adopt different age breakdowns to cater for specific demands. For example, results from the *New Earnings Survey* in the UK are presented in the following age breakdowns:

Under 18	25–29
50–59	
18–20	30–39
60–64	
21–24	40–49
65+	

Body Mass Index

The Body Mass Index (BMI) measures the weight of a person relative to their height. A BMI score of under 20 is defined as underweight, a BMI score of 20–25 is desirable, a BMI score of 25–30 is overweight, and a BMI score of over 30 is obese by definition.

Cohort

A cohort is a group of people sharing a common demographic experience; this group is observed through a period of time. For example, the male birth cohort of 1955 in Scotland consists of the males born in that year in Scotland.

Cohort analysis is the observation of the demographic behaviour of a given cohort through life, or through a specific time period: for example, examining the divorce rates of males born in 1955 in Scotland between 1980 and 2000. Rates derived from this cohort analysis are cohort measures.

Crude Rates

Crude rates measure the relative frequency of specific events (i.e. births, deaths, abortions, marriages, divorces, etc.) within the population as a whole in a specific period of time. They are usually calculated by dividing the number of events during a specific year by the average population. The resulting ratios are usually expressed per 1,000 inhabitants or per 1,000 residents, e.g. birth rates per 1,000 inhabitants, or marriages per 1,000 inhabitants.

Dependency Ratio

The dependency ratio is the ratio of the economically dependent part of the population to the productive part. The economically dependent part is usually defined as the elderly (those over retirement age) and the young (those under 15 years of age). The productive part is usually defined as the population of working age.

Enumerated Population

The enumerated population is the population figure taken at a specific census date.

Fertility Rate

The total fertility rate is usually defined as the average number of children that would be born alive to a woman during her lifetime if she were to pass through her childbearing years conforming to the age-specific fertility rates of a given year.

Life Expectancy

The life expectancy is the average number of additional years a person would live if current mortality trends were to continue.

Life Tables

Life tables show the probability of dying at each age for a given population according to the age-specific death rates prevailing at a given period. In the UK, life tables are calculated from the estimated population in a specific year and the number of deaths occurring in that year.

Migration

Migration is defined as the movement of people across a specific boundary for the purpose of establishing a new permanent residence. Migration can cover both internal population movements (within a country or geographical area) and international migration (between countries or regions).

International migration data for the UK is obtained from the International Passenger Survey (IPS) (see that entry in chapter 6). The IPS is a continuous survey with information on passengers entering or leaving the UK (excluding routes between the UK and the Irish Republic, the Channel Islands, Isle of Man, and the rest of the world). A migrant into the UK is defined as a person who has resided abroad for a year or more and states the intention to stay in the UK for a year or more. The opposite is true for a migrant from the UK.

Internal migration data for the UK are based on NHS doctors' patient movements between Family Health Services Authority Areas (FHSAs) in England and Wales and Area Health Boards in Scotland and Northern Ireland. Data based on FHSAs is currently being replaced by data based on Health Authorities (HAs) which have replaced FHSAs. When UK residents move, they register with a new doctor in a new area and these registrations form the basis for internal migration data.

Migration figures are found in general population statistics and titles and more detailed data is available in *Internal Migration* (quarterly) and *International Migration* (annual), both from National Statistics (see that entry and International Passenger Survey in chapter 6).

Net Migration

Net migration is the net effect of immigration and emigration on an area's population in a given time period, expressed as an increase or a decrease.

Population Census

A population census is usually a count of the total population and total households. In the UK, a full census has been held every 10 years since 1801 except in 1941, although a national register of the population was produced in 1939. The 1841 census is usually seen as the first modern census because, for the first time, households were asked to complete the census forms themselves and names and addresses were recorded. First results from the 2001 census (carried out on Sunday 29th April 2001) were published in September 2002 and more have followed since. See *www.statistics.gov.uk/census2001/default.asp* for more details. Preliminary results from the census are usually available within two or three months but the collection, analysis, and publication of more detailed results takes longer.

The UK census is not just a count of the population. It provides information on a range of topics including demographic characteristics, economic activity, housing, migration, travel and transport, household amenities, and health.

As well as national data on demographic trends and characteristics, and specific topics such as economic activity, and households, published output from the census also covers regions, counties, local authority areas, electoral wards, and enumeration districts (EDs). There are 148,212 EDs and the ED is the basic administrative unit for the census. An ED area typically has 175–225 households in it. National reports and reports for regions, counties, and local authorities have traditionally been published in hard copy format; ward and ED data is usually available electronically.

Many developed countries have a census every 10 years although there are exceptions. For example, Japan has a population census every five years. In some countries, it is a legal requirement to notify any change of address to a central or local register and, in these countries, very up-to-date population figures are produced from these registers. These figures are often produced monthly or quarterly. In these countries, the value of the census as the major count of the population is not as crucial as in countries such as the UK where the census offers the only real chance to measure the population accurately.

Population Density

The population density is the relationship between a population and the area in which it lives. The most basic population density measure is calculated by dividing the total population of an area (i.e. country, region, city, town) by the area of the territory and the density is usually expressed as the number of persons per square mile or per square kilometre. In Eurostat population data, a densely populated area is defined as an area with a population density exceeding 500 inhabitants per square kilometre (see Urbanisation).

Population Estimates

In the UK, national population estimates are produced annually along with estimates for regions, counties, local authority areas, and health authority areas. These estimates are mid-year estimates which use the census population data as the base year and update this data in subsequent years before the next census. The estimates take into account births, deaths, migration, plus any changes in the armed forces and dependents, and prisoners. Some other countries produce mid-year estimates; others produce end-year and beginning-year estimates. For example, Germany publishes mid-year and end-year estimates, France produces estimates for 1 January each year, and the US produces mid-year estimates. Some countries, such as the Netherlands, have population registers which are updated continuously and published data is available monthly.

The most difficult indicator to calculate is migration and various sources are used. International migration figures are available from the International Passenger Survey (IPS) (see that entry in chapter 6) but this is only based on a sample of passengers moving through ports and airports. Internal migration is calculated from two sources – the National and Health Service Central Register (and its equivalents in Scotland and Ireland) and changes in the numbers on local electoral rolls, although both these source still do not give a truly comprehensive picture. The accuracy of the former source depends on migrants registering with a new doctor and, although householders are obliged by law to supply data for the electoral roll, not all households do.

Population Projections

Population projections describe the expected trends in the population in future years. Population projections often include a high, medium, and low projection and these variants are often based on different assumptions regarding future fertility. The UK population projections produced by the Government Actuary's Department (GAD) are based on various assumptions concerning fertility, birth rates, death rates, and migration. The projections are based on the previous year's population estimates and UK projections are by age and sex for the next 70 years in five-year age bands.

UK population projections have been produced since 1919 and, between 1955 and 1979, national projections were produced every year. Since the 1980s, the national population projections have been produced every two years. GAD produces projections by marital status and the last version was published in 1996.

Sub-national population projections are produced for Government Office Regions, counties, local government areas, health regions, and health authorities.

World population projections by country are produced by the United Nations every two years with current projections by country, sex, and age band up to 2050. See *Long Range World Population Projections* in chapter 6. Eurostat produces population projections for the European

Union, and summary tables are found in the annual *Demographic Statistics* (see chapter 6).

Resident Population

The resident population refers to all residents living in a specific country or area, whatever their nationality. Nationals serving abroad in the armed forces are excluded but foreign nationals in the armed forces and based in the country concerned are included.

Small Area Statistics

Small Area Statistics (SAS) are population census statistics arranged by Enumeration Districts (EDs) (see Population Census). SAS are available for a range of local areas and are not published in a conventional sense but are available on request. Typical areas covers by SAS are enumeration districts, civil parishes, wards, and postcode sectors.

Specific Rates

Specific rates measure the relative frequency of a particular event within a subgroup of the population, for example abortions amongst teenage girls, as opposed to Crude Rates (see that entry), which apply to the population as a whole.

Urbanisation

Urban areas in UK official statistics are categorised as follows:

- London Borough – the 33 London boroughs
- Metropolitan built-up area – the built-up area within the administrative areas of the former metropolitan counties of Greater Manchester, Merseyside, the West Midlands, West Yorkshire, Tyne & Wear, and Strathclyde
- Large urban – self-contained urban area of more than 250,000 population in 1991
- Medium urban – self-contained urban area of not more than 250,000 population in 1991, but more than 25,000
- Small urban – self-contained urban area of not more than 25,000 population in 1991 but more than 3,000
- Rural – areas other than those above, including 'urban areas' under 3,000 population in 1991.

For international comparisons, definitions of urban areas and urbanisation can vary from country to country and international definitions may not be relevant to all countries. In Eurostat demographic statistics and demographic analysis, three types of area are identified: densely populated area; intermediate area; sparsely populated area. An 'area' consists of a group of contiguous 'local areas' such as wards in the UK, communes in France or Italy, or Gemeinde in Germany. The definitions are:

- Densely populated area – A contiguous set of local areas each with a population density exceeding 500 inhabitants per square kilometre, where the total population of the set is at least 50,000 inhabitants.

- Intermediate area – A contiguous set of local areas not belonging to a densely populated area, each local area with a population density exceeding 100 inhabitants per square kilometre, the set either having a total population of at least 50,000 inhabitants or lying adjacent to a densely populated area

- Thinly populated area – A contiguous set of local areas not forming part of a densely populated or intermediate area.

4

Business statistics

Business statistics provide information on the structure of economic activity within an economy and, at a more specific level, they can offer a profile of the structure of a specific sector or industry or even provide information on specific products and services. For specific industries and business and industry in general, there may be information available on areas such as the number of enterprises and establishments, production, output, turnover, sales, investment, purchases, stocks, employment, earnings, imports, and exports.

Traditionally, the UK has been a manufacturing economy and the official business statistics still reflect this with a strong emphasis on particular manufacturing sectors. There is also considerable data on agriculture, forestry and fishing, mining, energy, transport, and construction. In contrast, detailed published statistics on the growing service sector are still less comprehensive even though services now account for the majority of jobs in the economy. Retailing is well covered by statistics, and trends in the retail trade are used as a yardstick for confidence levels in the consumer economy. Coverage of other service industries is improving and Eurostat, the Statistical Office of the European Communities, has identified the service sector as a priority area for improved statistical surveys.

Business indicators

Agriculture

The term 'agriculture' in published statistics usually includes hunting, forestry, and fishing, as well as agriculture itself.

Business Demographics

Business demographics refers to the classification and demography of business and involves mapping the number of businesses in a specific sector or total economy, registering and analysing the births and deaths of businesses (i.e. business closures and business start-ups), and identifying the geographical distribution of businesses, etc.

Carry-in Sales

In official statistics, this refers to sales of products classified as principal to an industry which are made by a company classified to another industry (see Principal Products). One industry's carry-in sales are another industry's Carry-out Sales (see that entry).

Carry-out Sales

In official statistics, the production of non-principal products (see Principal Products) is known as carry-out sales as they are sales classified as principal to another industry. One industry's carry-out sales are another industry's Carry-in Sales (see that entry).

Construction Confidence Indicator

The Construction Confidence Indicator is the arithmetic average of the answers (balances) to the questions on order book and employment expectations in the Building Industry Business Survey carried out in EU member countries (see Opinion Polls and Business Surveys in chapter 5).

Construction Orders and Output

The construction sector is one of the most important sectors in the economy, and trends in this sector provide a guide to likely trends in the economy as a whole. The construction sector is a major employer in itself, but many other supplying industries also depend on it. Therefore, changes in economic and business conditions in the construction sector are important economic and business indicators. The main indicators for the construction sector are orders (these signal demand for building materials and labour over the coming months), and output. Both these indicators are usually expressed in both value and volume terms. The housing sector, a sub-sector of the construction industry, also has a number of indicators which offer a guide to general economic and business conditions (see Housing Statistics).

Deliveries

The term 'deliveries' in statistical tables usually refers to deliveries by manufacturers or other suppliers to the trade, i.e. distributors, wholesalers, and retailers.

Enterprise

An enterprise is the smallest combination of legal units that is an organisational unit producing goods or services. An enterprise can carry out one or more activities at one or more location. An enterprise may refer to legal units such as partnerships, limited companies, or plcs, etc.

Establishment

An establishment, as defined for national accounts purposes, is an enterprise or part of an enterprise that is situated in a single location and in which only a single production activity is carried out, or in which the principal production activity accounts for most of the value added.

Export Sales Ratio

An export sales ratio figure shows the extent to which exports contribute to sales in a specific domestic industry or product/service sector. For example, if the manufacturers in a specific country sell valves to the value of £278 million in a specific year and £62 million of this sales total is exported, then the export sales ratio is 22.3%, i.e. £62 million expressed as a percentage of £278 million. An export sales ratio can also be calculated for the sales of a specific company if that company has significant export sales.

Exports

Detailed information on products exported from the UK to countries outside the European Union (often described as extra-EU trade) are collected from customs records completed by exporters. Information on exports to other EU countries (often described as intra-EU trade) comes from the Intrastat system (see that entry in Chapter 1) and this creates a two-tier system of overseas trade information. Value and volume figures for individual product exports are included in the published monthly *Overseas Trade Statistics of the United Kingdom* and these exports are valued 'free on board' (FOB), i.e. excluding insurance premiums and freight (see FOB in chapter 7).

Housing Statistics

Statistics on housing starts, housing under construction, and housing completions are indicators of construction activity, a key sector of the economy. Statistics are available monthly, quarterly and annually in series such as *Housing and Construction Statistics* and *Local Housing Sta-*

tistics (see those entries in chapter 6). The number of housing starts gives an indication of the level of demand for construction materials, labour, and construction services over the coming months. Housing under construction data gives an indication of the rate of progress and the number of new houses coming on to the market. Housing completion implies a house sale, a new mortgage, and increased consumer spending on household furniture, durables, and carpets and fittings.

Import Penetration

An import penetration figure shows the extent to which imports contribute to a specific national market, industry or product/service sector. For example, if the market for valves is valued at £340 million in a specific country and imports of valves into that country are valued at £177 million, then import penetration in the valve market is 52%, i.e. £177 million expressed as a percentage of the total market value of £340 million.

Imports

Detailed information on products imported into the UK from outside the EU (often described as extra-EU trade) are collected from customs records completed by importers and others. Information on imports from other EU countries (often described as intra-EU trade) comes from the Intrastat system (see that entry in chapter 1) and this creates a two-tier system of overseas trade information. Value and volume figures for individual product imports are included in the published monthly *Overseas Trade Statistics of the United Kingdom* and these imports are valued including insurance and freight (see CIF in chapter 7).

Index of Industrial Production

The Index of Industrial Production (IOP) measures the volume of production at constant prices for the production industries in the UK. The production industries cover mining and quarrying, manufacturing, and utilities. The IOP is published monthly with data for total industrial production and for specific sectors.

It is a useful short-term guide to trends in UK economic output but it only covers the production industries which now account for less than 30% of UK output. Industrial production tables are published in monthly editions of the *Monthly Digest of Statistics* and are also available monthly as *Industrial Production Statistical Release*.

Index of Producer Prices of Agricultural Products

The Index of Producer Prices of Agricultural Products is a specific price index for core agricultural produce.

Index of Purchaser Prices of the Means of Agricultural Production

The Index of Purchaser Prices of the Means of Agricultural Production is a price index for various farm inputs and purchases including energy products, feedstuffs, and machinery.

Index of Services

In April 2000, National Statistics began the first phase of a programme to develop a detailed monthly Index of Services to reflect the importance of the service sector, and to parallel the monthly Index of Industrial Production. A prototype series has been launched, see *www.statistics.gov.uk/themes/economy/articles/shorttermindicators/ios.asp*.

Industrial Confidence Indicator

The Industrial Confidence Indicator is the arithmetic average of the answers (balances) to the questions on production, order books, and stocks expectations in the Manufacturing Industry Business Survey carried out in EU member countries (see Opinion Polls and Business Surveys in chapter 5).

Industry

'Industry' in published statistics usually covers mining and quarrying, manufacturing, utilities, and construction.

International Trade

International trade covers the trade in goods and services between different countries or trading areas. Imports are goods and services brought into an economy from outside its boundaries; exports are goods and services sold outside the boundaries of an economy (see Exports and Imports). Trade in goods is sometimes referred to as merchandise trade. Trade data is collected on the basis of a country's customs area, which in most cases is the same as its geographical area.

Collecting and tabulating trade data is complicated by various factors. Information is often collected at customs points when individual importers and exporters are required to fill in the necessary forms. Where forms are completed incorrectly, this can affect trade data. The time lags and complexities involved in international trade mean that it is inadvisable to compare one country's export data to a specific country with the destination country's import data from the original country. According to the published data, a certain amount of product A may appear to have been imported into country X, but country X may not actually have imported this amount. All or some of the amount may have been re-exported by country X to another country. Some may have been kept in storage for a long period. Imports into country X from country Y may also have initially originated from another country.

Some developing countries lack the resources to produce regular trade data and, in these instances, their trade is often estimated from the data reported by their trading partners. Some countries suppress international trade data for certain products such as oil or military and defence equipment. If one company dominates exports then figures may be suppressed to maintain confidentiality. In some countries and regions, smuggling and black market trading mean that many trade flows remain unreported.

See also Balance of Payments and Terms of Trade in chapter 2.

Kind of Activity Unit

The Kind of Activity Unit (KAU) is a concept used in Eurostat business statistics and it groups all the parts of an enterprise that contribute to the performance of an activity at class level (four-digit level) of NACE (see that entry in chapter 1).

Local Unit

A local unit is part of an enterprise or enterprises situated in a geographically identified place and classified according to its main activity.

Manufacturer's Sales

UK official statistics on sales by industry and products/services usually refer to manufacturer's sales. These refer to all sales, including sales destined for export markets as well as the home market. The figures are usually based on a sample of companies in a specific sector based on a Minimum Threshold (see that entry in chapter 7) below which companies are not included in the sample. Estimates are made for companies excluded from the sample and the final sales figures refer to all companies in the sector not just those in the survey.

Published figures can be value figures (in £million) and/or volume figures by units, or weight. The term 'manufacturer's shipments' may be used in some countries (e.g. USA) and these terms usually have the same meaning as manufacturer's sales.

As manufacturer's sales figures include exports, but exclude imports, they can not be used as a measure of the size of a specific domestic market. Other measures such as retail sales, or Apparent Consumption (see entry Net Supply in chapter 7) are more appropriate.

Price Adjustment Formulae

Price Adjustment Formulae were established by the National Economic Development Office (NEDO) in 1973 and they are still often referred to as 'the NEDO Indices'. They are a series of price indices published for labour and work done in the construction industry. They are published monthly by the Department of the Environment, Transport and the Regions (DETR) as *Price Adjustment Formulae – Monthly Bulletin of Indices*.

Principal Products

All companies in the UK are classified to a five-digit sub-sector of the Standard Industrial Classification (SIC) (see that entry in chapter 1) according to their main economic activity. Principal products are those classified to an industry and are products mainly produced by firms classified to that industry.

Production

Production statistics usually refer to either manufacturing production or industrial production. Although there may be differences in definitions between countries, and it is worth checking on these, manufacturing production data usually covers the value-added output of manufacturing companies. Industrial production usually covers manufacturing production plus construction, the supply of energy and water, and the output of mines, oil wells and fields, and quarries. Industrial production usually excludes agriculture, forestry, fisheries, and service sectors.

Retail Sales Index

The Retail Sales Index is based on a sample survey of the UK's main retailers. It is published monthly in index form, in both current prices and constant prices. It covers all forms of spending in retail outlets, but other consumer spending and spending in the retail motor trade is excluded. It is a useful indicator of short-term trends in consumer spending, although retail sales now only represent around 35% of total consumer spending. Consumer spending on other areas such as leisure activities, holidays, financial services, etc. has grown in recent years and reduced the percentage of total consumer expenditure spent in retail outlets. The monthly figures for the index can be volatile with holidays (e.g. Christmas, Easter), the timing of sales, and the weather (hot weather depresses sales) affecting retail sales.

Sales

Various sales measures are published regularly, but these series are not directly comparable. Key sales series are Manufacturer's Sales and the Retail Sales Index (see those entries). There are also sales figures for key sectors of the economy, which can provide a guide to trends in the economy as a whole, for example house sales or car sales.

Services

Services in published statistics usually covers the wholesale and retail trade; restaurants, hotels, and catering; transport and travel; communications; financial services; real estate; business services; and community, social, and personal services.

Shipments

Shipments is often used as an alternative term for Manufacturer's Sales (see that entry). It is a common terminology in US manufacturing data.

Stocks

Stocks (sometimes referred to as inventories) are goods or commodities held in storage which have yet to be sold on to the market. Changes in stocks indicators refer to the differences in stock levels at the end of a specific reference period compared with stock levels at the beginning of the reference period. Stocks can accumulate when there is a sharp downturn in demand and, when demand increases, there may be a sudden fall in stocks.

Manufacturing output figures for a specific product or sector may not match sales figures in that market or sector for many reasons and one reason is that stocks may be accumulating or stocks may be falling. The stocks : sales ratios at each stage of economic activity (manufacturing, wholesaling, retailing) are significant leading indicators. If the ratios are higher than normal (in comparison with a long run of figures), this suggests that production and imports will be cut unless demand increases. If the ratios are lower than normal, the implication is that production and imports will rise unless demand falls.

5

Market and media data

The market research and media research industries have created a vast array of research and survey techniques as well as statistical and market data definitions and terminologies, and these are described here.

Surveys may be ad-hoc or continuous and consider either consumer or business-to-business markets. The main types of surveys include attitude surveys, audience surveys, consumer panels, home audits, omnibus surveys, opinion polls, readership surveys, retail audits, and tracking surveys; all these are described in this chapter.

Market research terminology

Above-the-line Advertising

'Above-the-line' is the term used for advertising in traditional commission-paying media such as the press (newspapers, journals, and magazines), TV, radio, cinema, outdoor, and poster advertising. Published advertising expenditure data is often based on advertising spending through the above media. See also Below-the-line Advertising.

Ad-Hoc Survey

An ad-hoc survey is a one-off survey or single piece of research designed for a specific purpose and usually carried out during a particular time period. This contrasts with a continuous survey (see Continuous Surveys) or surveys repeated or carried out at regular intervals.

Attitude Research

Attitude research investigates the attitudes of people towards specific products, campaigns, issues, services, or organisations, etc.

Audience Share

Audience share research analyses the percentage of the total viewing audience viewing a specific TV channel.

Audience Surveys

Audience surveys measure audiences primarily for TV, radio, and cinema. The survey results are used not only by the media companies but also by the advertising industry.

Average Issue Readership

The average issue readership is the average number of people who see an issue of a newspaper, journal, magazine, newsletter, or other regular publications.

Base

In market research, the term base usually refers to the number of respondents answering each question in a questionnaire.

Behavioural Research

Behavioural research investigates human behaviour, i.e. what people do as opposed to what they think. Behavioural research can be undertaken on an individual or on a group and it is often related to buying or consumption habits. It may also be used to consider wider social issues.

Below-the-line Advertising

'Below-the-line' is the term used for advertising where the advertising agency obtains a fee. Below-the-line advertising includes direct mail, sponsorship, public relations, sales promotions, or merchandising. See also Above-the-line Advertising

Brand Awareness

Brand Awareness indicates the extent to which a brand or brand name is recognised by buyers and potential buyers, and correctly associated with the right product. It is often monitored by tracking studies. Research looking for unprompted or spontaneous brand awareness will ask questions such as 'Which brands of frozen ready meals can you think of?' Prompted awareness is measured by showing a list of brands and asking respondents if they have heard of these brands.

Business Surveys

See Opinion Polls and Business Surveys.

Business-to-business Surveys

The term 'business-to-business' denotes surveys and research projects relating to business sectors and markets rather than consumer markets. For example, surveys may cover purchases by businesses, or sales to businesses.

Consumer Durables

Consumer durables are bought occasionally by consumers, usually for the house, and are consumed over a long period of time. They usually have a life cycle of three years or more. Examples include 'white goods', such as washing machines, fridges, and freezers and 'brown goods', such as TVs, radios, and CD players. Government surveys such as the General Household Survey and Family Expenditure Survey (see those entries in chapter 6), plus various market research surveys, have ownership figures for selected consumer durables usually expressed as the percentage of households owning a specific consumer durable.

Consumer Panel

A consumer panel is a sample of individuals who are surveyed over a period of time, perhaps at regular intervals, to consider areas such as their purchases, their product usage, and media use. A consumer panel enables the same sample of consumers to be surveyed over time and results can identify changes in purchases, habits, and use.

Continuous Surveys

Continuous surveys are carried out on a continuing basis, or are regularly repeated at frequent intervals. Retail audits, consumer panels, and tracking studies are examples. The major UK government surveys such as the Family Expenditure Survey and General Household Survey (see these entries in chapter 6) are also continuous.

Cover

The cover, sometimes expressed as the coverage or reach, of a single advertisement is the percentage of the target audience to whom it is exposed.

Fast Moving Consumer Goods

Fast moving consumer goods (FMCGs) are products that are regularly purchased and used by consumers and are subject to frequent repeat purchases. Stocks of these goods in retail outlets need to be replenished at very frequent intervals. Many food, drink, and cosmetic and toiletries markets, for example, are FMCG markets.

Focus Group

Focus groups, or group discussions, are a method used in qualitative research and surveys. Groups of people are brought together and a moderator leads the group through a discussion on a specific area or topic. The topic could be a specific social or economic issue, a brand or product, or an issue specific to the particular focus group selected.

Hall Test

A hall test is a research activity in which people participating in the research are invited into a specific location, such as a hall, to answer questions.

Home Audit

A home audit uses a panel of households and this panel is used to undertake regular measurements of purchases and consumption. A home audit can use various methods to collect the data including the completion of a diary, interviews, or dustbin checks.

Horizontal Market

Horizontal market surveys and research consider buyers from various sectors and groups but these buyers are purchasing or consuming a common product or service. For example, a survey of purchasers of office photocopying machinery may consider buyers from various industries buying the same product.

Lifestyle Surveys

Lifestyle surveys can categorise consumers or communities on the basis of specific personality traits, interests and opinions, behavioural patterns, or even the types of products and services consumed. A number of lifestyle classifications have been developed for commercial use, and these are described in chapter 1.

Market Map

A market map shows the relative positions of selected brands in terms of the most important brand characteristics.

Market Penetration

See Penetration.

Market Profile

See Profile.

Market Segmentation

Market segmentation involves dividing a market into specific parts; each part has identifiable characteristics. Segmentation may be based on the characteristics of the product, or on the characteristics of the purchasers or users. Market segmentation is used to identify new or growing markets, target products and services more precisely, and improve market performance.

Segmentation based on product characteristics, for example, might break the frozen food market into frozen ready meals, frozen fish products, frozen pizzas, frozen vegetables, frozen poultry and so on, or it might segment by product price, i.e. premium, standard, and economy products. Segmentation based on purchaser characteristics might segment the frozen food market by age bands of purchasers, household characteristics of purchasers, or income group of purchasers, etc.

Market Share

Market share is to the proportion of a market accounted for by a specific brand, company, or other supplier. It is usually expressed as either: a value market share, i.e. share of the total value of the market taken by a specific brand or company; or a volume market share, i.e. share of the total volume of the market (numbers sold for example) taken by a specific brand or company.

Media Research

Media research involves research into the readership of print media, or research into audiences for TV, radio, and cinema.

Multi-client Research

Multi-client research, sometimes referred to as syndicated research, is research where the costs and survey results are shared among a number of clients.

Mystery Shopping Surveys

The collection of information from retail outlets and other sites used by consumers by researchers posing as ordinary members of the public.

Neighbourhood Classifications

Neighbourhood classifications, or geo-demographic classifications, are used to classify neighbourhoods of similar types for geo-demographic research. See entry Geo-demographic Classifications in chapter 1.

Omnibus Surveys

An omnibus survey usually covers a number of different topics, and different clients can add their own specific questions to the survey. These questions and their answers are confidential to the client. Omnibus surveys are usually carried out at regular intervals, perhaps weekly, monthly, or quarterly, and they are called omnibus surveys because individual clients can 'hop on' to the survey with specific questions, the equivalent of hopping on to an omnibus. With most omnibus surveys, it is possible to join the survey at a particular time with a specific question or questions without having to be a regular client of the survey. A fee is normally charged per question.

There are various consumer omnibus surveys and also some business-to-business omnibus surveys. The results from consumer omnibus surveys are usually available within a few days of the completion of the survey.

Opinion Polls and Business Surveys

Opinion polls are normally associated with political opinion polls where samples of individuals are canvassed for their opinions on political parties, policies, and issues. While the number of political opinion polls has increased in recent years, opinion polls and opinion surveys are also used for many other purposes including finding out people's attitudes and opinions on products and services, topical issues, and social trends. Opinion surveys are used in many business sectors to obtain opinions from senior executives and managers on likely trends in a specific business sector. They are also being increasingly used to assess consumer confidence and likely consumer spending trends.

Opinion surveys of business executives can offer an early indication of changes in specific sectors or changes in the overall business climate. Business executives are asked about their expectations for their own business and for the sector as a whole usually for the next three months, six months, or 12 months. They may be asked questions about their expectations regarding future sales, investment, employment, prices, stocks, or exports. The individual responses to each question are aggregated and the aggregate result of the replies to a specific question is usually expressed as a 'balance'. This balance is the difference between the number or percentage of respondents replying positively to a question and the number replying negatively. For example, a positive answer might be, 'sales are going to increase in the next six months', or 'I am more optimistic about the climate for investment in the next six months' whereas a negative answer might be, 'sales are going to decrease in the next six months', or 'I am very pessimistic about the climate for investment in the next six months'.

The *CBI Industrial Trends Survey* (see *European Economy Supplement B – Business and Consumer Survey Results*) is based on an opinion survey across various sectors, but there are many other business opinion surveys for specific sectors particularly in the construction and retailing sectors. The CBI survey is part of a harmonised series of business opinion surveys across the EU and the results of all these surveys are published regularly by Eurostat. These include surveys of manufacturing, building industry, and retail trade (see *European Economy Supplement B – Business and Consumer Survey Results*).

There is also a harmonised series of consumer surveys across the EU which asks consumers about their expectations of their financial situation, the general economic situation, price changes, savings, and the likelihood of any major purchases. The results of all these surveys are also published by Eurostat.

The consumer confidence indicator, the construction confidence indicator, and the industrial confidence indicator are all arithmetic averages of various answers (balances) in each of these surveys.

Penetration

Penetration in market research refers to the proportion of a population or sub-group that has a certain characteristic. In consumer research, for example, it is often used to show the proportion of consumers, households, or some other population that buys or owns a specific product, brand, or service. For example:

- 51% of households buy frozen fish fingers
- 70% of shoppers aged between 25 and 35 buy frozen fish fingers
- 33% of single person households buy frozen fish fingers

- 98% of households have a colour TV.

Penetration is one way of assessing the potential for further growth in the market. A market with a high penetration, for example, is likely to be a mature market where further growth prospects may be limited. Low penetration levels, however, may suggest that there are opportunities for further growth in the market.

Published results from the Target Group Index (see entry in chapter 6) provide detailed penetration results annually for numerous consumer goods and services.

Profile

A profile in market research provides a profile or a breakdown of the users, purchasers, or owners of a specific product, brand, or service. In a consumer market, for example, a consumer profile might refer to the percentage of the population buying a particular product who are men or women, or break down purchasers by age group: for example, 36% of purchasers are aged between 25 and 34, 28% are aged between 35 and 44, 12% are over 65, and so on. In business-to-business surveys, an example could be a buyer profile that breaks down purchasers of office equipment into commercial, government, and further education purchasers. Published results from the Target Group Index (see that entry in chapter 6) provide detailed consumer profiles annually for numerous consumer goods and services.

Readership Surveys

Readership surveys are concerned with the number of people reading a specific title, as opposed to how many people purchase a specific title. These surveys provide useful information not only for the publishers but also for the advertising industry and the surveys often have broader information on the media usage of readers, their socio-economic backgrounds, budgets, and purchases.

Retail Audits

Retail audits are audits of a fixed sample of retail stores at regular intervals. These may be audits of consumer purchases, stocks, or prices. The traditional survey method was to visit the outlets included in the audit, but the widespread use of electronic point of sale (EPOS) equipment means that these surveys can now be completed electronically.

Saturation

The saturation of a market is the level at which its further expansion is unlikely without some segmentation of the market, or significant population growth and new users/purchasers, or significant replacement sales.

Syndicated Research

Syndicated research, sometimes referred to as multi-client research, is research where the costs and results of the research are shared between various clients.

Tracking Survey

A tracking survey is a continuous or regular survey tracking the use, awareness of, and attitudes to specific products, services, brands, companies, or organisations. The surveys often use the same questions and methodologies over time in order to monitor change.

Vertical Market

Vertical market surveys research products or services sold to one type of classification of market.

6

Selected statistical surveys and sources

The emphasis of this guide is on the understanding of statistical indicators and concepts. It was never the intention to produce a detailed guide to statistical sources and publications. Nevertheless, some of the core UK and international sources are listed here and, where appropriate, references have been made to these sources in the relevant entries in specific chapters. Also included here are the main statistical publishing bodies and survey organisations in the UK, as well as some selected international organisations.

In recent months, National Statistics has been active in offering more of their statistical titles and services as free files on the Web. This trend is set to continue and some titles are now only available as Web files. In the list of titles and services given in this chapter, URLs for specific sources are given where appropriate. Most of these URLs have details of the publications and links to downloadable PDF files of recent issues. New titles are being added to the Web regularly so it is worth checking the Bookshelf pages on *www.statistics.gov.uk* for the latest information. Where certain titles are not yet on the Web, it may be possible to find specific time series and datasets from the Statbase database on the Web. Details are given here under Statbase.

In the UK, there are a number of statistics users' groups which provide forums for discussion and debate about statistical issues, and offer collective voices for users of government statistics in specific sectors. These groups are listed in this chapter, and Appendix 3 has further contact details.

More detailed information on statistical publications and services in the UK can be obtained from two regularly updated sources:

* official statistics – *Guide to Official Statistics*. National Statistics. 2000 (also available free on the National Statistics Web site, at: *www.statistics.gov.uk/products/p1551.asp*).

* non-governmental statistics – *Sources of Unofficial UK Statistics*, 5th edition. Gower Publishing. 2002, at: *www.gowerpub.com*.

Key statistical sources, publishing bodies, and other organisations

199- Based National Population Projections

The national population projections are published every two years with details of the Government Actuary Department's population projections by age and sex for the UK. UK projections cover the next 70 years. The latest projections are available on the Web at *www.statistics.gov.uk/products/p4611.asp*.

Agricultural and Horticultural Census

The Agricultural and Horticultural Census is undertaken annually in the UK and is based on a sample of approximately 235,000 farms. *Agricultural Census Statistics for the UK* (replaced previously titled *Digest of Agricultural Census Statistics UK*) published by the Department of Environment, Food and Regional Affairs (DEFRA) provides key results. Since the 1998 report, it has been available only on the Web at *www.defra.gov.uk/esg/work_htm/publications/cs/census/census.htm*.

Annual Abstract of Statistics

The *Annual Abstract of Statistics* is an annual compendium of data from National Statistics covering the main economic, business, demographic, and social statistics. There are references to more detailed sources of information.

Annual Business Inquiry (Production and Construction)

The Annual Business Inquiry (ABI) is carried out by National Statistics, and samples UK businesses according to their employment size and industry sector. The survey covers sales, numbers employed, work done, services rendered, running costs, capital expenditure, and stocks. It is the major survey of UK economic structure and data is available nationally and for standard regions and local areas. The survey was originally established in 1907 as the Census of Production and was a five-yearly survey until it became annual in 1970. Provisional results are usually published 12 months after the survey year and revised details are available 18 months after the survey year. Detailed results are published in *PACSTAT Production and Construction Statistics* CD-ROM and summary results are in *Production and Construction Inquiries – Summary Volume*. Results are also available for specific industries.

Annual Employment Survey

The Annual Employment Survey (AES) is conducted annually in September to measure the number of employee jobs. The survey samples around 450,000 local units covering one-third of the work sites in the UK. From April 2001, the AES was replaced by the Annual Business Inquiry (ABI) as the source of information on employee jobs. The last AES covers the year 1998 and the ABI has been used from the survey year 1999 onwards. Available on disc from National Statistics, the Annual Employment Survey 1998 contains results analysed by industry, region, local area, and size band.

Annual Sample Survey of Production Industries

The Annual Sample Survey of Production Industries provides information on the structure of industry in the UK. Contributors for the survey are selected under a stratified random sampling scheme and the strata used are industry and employment size group. The sample sizes vary from industry to industry but minimum employment thresholds mean that smaller enterprises are largely excluded. All the larger enterprises in each industry are selected.

Blue Book

The Blue Book is the name given to the annual United Kingdom National Accounts publication (see *UK National Accounts – the Blue Book*).

British Business Survey

The British Business Survey is an annual survey sponsored by the media owners and operated by the British Media Research Committee. The survey examines readership patterns of business managers and executives and data analyses includes readership by demographic group, by occupation, by industry, and by involvement in decision-making process. Based on a sample of around 2,000, the survey covers the major business publications plus trade press specific to a particular industry or sector. The survey field work is open to tender and is currently being undertaken by research agency IPSOS-RSL Ltd. An annual survey report is available for purchase. Further details are at *www.ipsos.rslmedia.co.uk*.

British Crime Survey

The British Crime Survey has been conducted biennially by the Home Office in England and Wales since 1982. From 2001, the survey has become annual. The sampling frame is the Postcode Address File and around 20,000 households were included in the 2000 sample. This has been doubled to 40,000 households from 2001 onwards. The survey has data on the number of crimes committed, type of offences, type of victim, frequency of crimes, and crime prevention, and there are ad-hoc questions relating to attitudes to the police, drugs, etc. The survey is carried out in the first six months of the year and results are published towards the end of the year in statistical releases and reports. Details and access to data are at *www.homeoffice.gov.uk/rds/bcs/.html*.

British Household Panel Survey

The British Household Panel Survey is an annual survey using a sample of around 5,000 households and interviewing all adults in the sample households in Great Britain.

British Social Attitudes Survey

The British Social Attitudes Survey is an annual survey undertaken and published by the National Centre for Social Research, an independent non-profit-making research institute. First produced in 1983, it is based on a sample of around 3,600 households and the survey considers British social, economic, political, and moral values. The sampling frame is the Postcode Address File and the geographic coverage is Great Britain. One adult in each household is surveyed. The results are published in *British Social Attitudes*.

Broadcasters Audience Research Board

The Broadcasters Audience Research Board (BARB) monitors television viewing habits and trends in the UK. BARB data covers terrestrial, cable, and satellite TV, and the survey data is obtained from a sample of 11,000 respondents who provide data on viewing habits from an electronic meter fitted to their TV. The core output is a weekly audience report and a general press release. More detailed analysis is available for clients. Further details and top-line data is at *www.barb.co.uk*.

Building Trust in Statistics

The Building Trust in Statistics white paper sets out the framework for quality assured national statistics in the UK.

Business Counts

National Statistics compiles annual data on the number of businesses in the UK and categorises these businesses by sizeband, location, and industry. The data is taken from the Inter-departmental Business Register (IDBR) and the information has been published since 1971. The data is collected around the middle of the year and published in *Size Analysis of UK Businesses* before the end of the year.

Business Statistics Users' Group

The Business Statistics Users' Group (BSUG) is a forum for users of official business statistics.

Capital Expenditure Inquiry

The Quarterly Capital Expenditure Inquiry from National Statistics is based on a sample of 16,000 businesses in the UK. Grossed results are estimated using the total population of businesses on the Inter-departmental Business Register (IBRD).

Catering and Allied Trades Inquiry

This annual inquiry from National Statistics is a sample survey covering around 4,200 businesses, which was first carried out in the mid-1950s. The results are published within 18 months of the survey year in *Sector Review: Catering and Allied Trades*.

Census of Population

See Population Census in chapter 3.

Census of Production

See Annual Business Inquiry.

Comext

Comext is a database of external trade information maintained by Eurostat. The database has detailed import and export information for approximately 5,000 products. Trade between EU countries and trade between EU countries and non-EU countries is included. Eurostat Data Shops can answer inquiries on import and export data from Comext. Further information is at *www.datashop.org/en/comexten.html*.

Commodity Trade Database

The Commodity Trade database (COMTRADE) is maintained by the United Nations Statistics Division and is based on an international agreement whereby member countries report their customs data to the UN.

Computer Services Survey

The Computer Services Survey is a pilot survey conducted by the Office for National Statistics collecting sales by type of service 'product'. Conducted in 2000, this is the first official source of detailed service sector sales by product. The survey is part of a feasibility exercise into the possibilities of a SERVCOM inquiry similar to the existing PRODCOM inquiry (see PRODCOM in chapter 1). Data from the survey is available at *www.statistics.gov.uk/products/p6869.asp*.

Construction Industry Survey

A monthly construction industry survey is carried out in 15 EU member countries to elicit opinions on production, order book, employment, and price trends and expectations. The general results are published in *European Economy Series B – Business and Consumer Survey Results* from the Office for Official Publications of the European Communities.

Construction Output – GB

The Department of Trade and Industry (DTI) collects returns of construction activity (output and employment) from a sample taken from a VAT-based register. Estimates are made for smaller firms and self-employed workers not on the register. Data is collected quarterly and annually. Details and data freely available at *www.dti.gov.uk/construction/stats/output.htm*.

Consumer Price Indices

The Consumer Price Indices are monthly reports on general consumer prices and prices of specific goods and services, available from National Statistics. Published in *Focus on Consumer Price Indices* available on the Bookshelf pages of *www.statistics.gov.uk*.

Consumer Surveys

Monthly consumer surveys are undertaken in 14 EU countries (they are not undertaken in Luxembourg), and these elicit opinions on the financial situation of households, future purchases and savings, and the general economic situation. The general results are published in *European Economy Series B – Business and Consumer Survey Results* published by the Office for Official Publications of the European Communities.

Consumer Trends

Consumer Trends is a quarterly title from National Statistics with detailed tables covering household consumption expenditure in general, and on specific product and service categories. From September 2001, the publication has only been available on the government statistics Web site and the hard copy version is no longer published. For details and links to data, visit *www.statistics.gov.uk/products/p242.asp.*

Criminal Justice Statistics Forum

The Criminal Justice Statistics Forum (CJSF) is a forum for users of official crime data.

Cronos

See New Cronos.

Databank

See National Statistics DataBank.

Data Archive

The Data Archive at the University of Essex offers the largest UK collection of computer-readable data on social and economic topics. Data comes from government, and academic sources, commercial surveys, and datasets and these are primarily available to the research community and teachers. The Data Archive has over 5,000 datasets. Further information regarding surveys and datasets at *www.data-archive.ac.uk.*

Demographic Statistics

Demographic Statistics is an annual publication from Eurostat, the Statistical Office of the European Communities, containing the principal demographic series for the EU and its member countries.

Development of the Oil and Gas Resources of the UK

Often referred to as the 'Brown Book', *Development of the Oil and Gas Resources of the UK* is an annual source of data on the UK's oil and gas resources. It is published by the Department of Trade and Industry (DTI), and there is free Web access to the latest edition at *www.dbd-data.co.uk/bb2001/*.

Digest of Data for the Construction Industry

The *Digest of Data for the Construction Industry* is an annual digest of constructions statistics. Free Web access to construction data is available at *www.dti.gov.uk/construction/stats/index.htm*.

Digest of UK Energy Statistics

Published by the DTI, the *Digest of UK Energy Statistics* has data for the latest five years on production, consumption, trade, and prices for specific energy sectors. It is available free on the Web at *www.dti.gov.uk/epa/dukes.htm*.

Domestic Acquisitions and Mergers Inquiry

The Domestic Acquisitions and Mergers Inquiry is an inquiry from National Statistics detailing the numbers and value of acquisitions and mergers in the UK. The inquiry is voluntary and businesses are approached only when there are press details of relevant transactions to report. It is a continuous survey, with the results published quarterly.

Economic Trends

Economic Trends is a monthly digest of economic data produced by National Statistics. Many tables include up to five years of data as well as recent figures. Regular articles on economic issues and data are also included.

Economic Trends Annual Supplement Historical

The *Economic Trends Annual Supplement Historical* provides UK economic data for 30–40 years, as well as notes on the definitions and methodologies used in compiling UK economic statistics.

Education and Training Statistics Users' Group

The Education and Training Statistics Users' Group (ETSUG) provides a forum for users of official education and training statistics.

Employers Skills Survey

The Employers Skills Survey is an annual survey of employers based on 26,952 interviews in England in the latest year.

Energy Trends

Energy Trends is a monthly statistical bulletin covering the UK energy sector, published by Department of Trade and Industry (DTI). It is available free on the Web along with other regular titles at URL: *www.dti.gov.uk/energy/energystats/energystats.htm*.

English House Condition Survey

Undertaken every five years, the English House Condition Survey uses the Postcode Address File as the sampling frame. The sample is around 27,000 addresses in England and the aim of the survey is to monitor the housing stock. The latest survey is 2001 and results are usually published 18 months after the completion of the fieldwork.

Enterprises in Europe

Enterprises in Europe, published by Eurostat, offers a detailed analysis of the structure of industry in the EU with details of companies, an analysis by industry and country, and SME analysis. The sixth edition was published in 2001.

Eurobarometer

Established in 1973, Eurobarometer public opinion surveys are conducted on behalf of DG X of the European Commission in spring and autumn each year and published twice a year. The home page of the Eurobarometer survey is at *www.europa.eu.int/en/comm/dg10/infcom/epo/eb.html*.

European Community Household Panel Survey

The European Community Household Panel Survey is a standardised annual survey undertaken in all EU member countries. The survey covers approximately 60,000 households and all adults over 16 are asked to take part. It includes details of household characteristics, incomes, and expenditure, etc. See also the British Household Panel Survey.

European Economy Supplement A – Economic Trends

The *European Economy Supplement A – Economic Trends* is published 11 times a year, with economic trends, and forecasts in some issues, for EU member countries.

European Economy Supplement B – Business And Consumer Survey Results

European Economy Series B – Business and Consumer Survey Results is published 11 times a year and contains the results of the business and consumer surveys carried out using a standard methodology in EU member countries. Specific surveys cover manufacturing, construction, investment, retail trade, and consumers.

Europe in Figures

Europe in Figures is a CD-ROM with data on Europe's economy, and political and social status. The CD-ROM is updated annually and has downloadable tables and text.

Europroms

Europroms is a database of product statistics maintained by Eurostat and based on the PRODCOM classification of products (see PRODCOM in chapter 1). There are statistics on approximately 5,000 product headings. Eurostat Data Shops can answer inquiries for product statistics from this database.

Eurostatistics

Eurostatistics is a monthly statistical title from Eurostat covering the key economic indicators for member states and the EU as a whole. The data is taken from the New Cronos database (see that entry).

Eurostat Data Shops

Eurostat Data Shops are access points for most Eurostat publications and for customised statistical inquiries. The Data Shops are found in all EU member countries and other countries such as USA and Japan. A full list of Data Shops is available on the Eurostat Web site, at *www.europa.eu.int/comm/eurostat*.

Eurostat Yearbook

The *Eurostat Yearbook* is an annual statistical compilation from Eurostat with indicators for member countries and the EU as a whole for the last 10 years. It is divided into five main themes: the people, the land and the environment, and national income and expenditure; enterprises and activities in Europe, and the European Union.

Expenditure and Food Survey

Launched on 1 April 2001, the Expenditure and Food Survey (EFS) merges two previously separate surveys – the National Food Survey and the Family Expenditure Survey (see those entries). Data collection and validation for the two surveys is now combined to improve methodologies and reduce overlap and costs. Results for food and drink expenditure will continue to be published separately.

Family Expenditure Survey

The Family Expenditure Survey (FES) is a continuous survey in the UK of household expenditure (with some household income data). This National Statistics survey has been conducted each year since 1957. The sampling frame is based on the Postcode Address File in Great Britain and the Rating and Valuation Lists in Northern Ireland. The sample is over 11,000 households, and response is voluntary. Each individual aged over 16 in households selected is asked to keep a diary of daily expenditure over a two-week period. Information about other expenditure, such as rent and mortgage payments and expenditure on large, infrequent items such as vehicles, is obtained during a household interview.

A detailed breakdown of household expenditure and income is published annually in the survey report *Family Spending*. This contains detailed analyses of expenditure on goods and services by household income, composition, size, type, and location. However, it is published almost a year after the year to which it relates. It is available free on the Web at *www.statistics.gov.uk/products/p361.asp*. More up-to-date detailed information can be obtained from National Statistics for a fee, and 'top line' up-to-date data is published in a quarterly press release.

From 1 April 2001, the data collection and validation phases of the Family Expenditure Survey merged with the National Food Survey (see that entry). This improves the data collection process and costs less than the two surveys separately. The new survey is called the

Expenditure and Food Survey (EFS) (see that entry), but results for food and drink will continue to be published separately.

Family Resources Survey

The Family Resources Survey is a continuous survey based on a sample of over 34,000 households in Great Britain taken from the Postcode Address File. All adults in each survey household are included in the survey. Originally an internal survey undertaken by the Department of Social Security (DSS), the survey is now available generally and has information on household characteristics, income and benefit receipt, tenure and housing costs, assets and savings, carers, occupation, and employment. It is published annually as *Family Resources Survey*. The latest report is available free on the Web at *www.dss.gov.uk/publications/dss/2001/frs/index.htm*.

Family Spending

Family Spending is the annual report of the Family Expenditure Survey (FES) with a breakdown of household expenditure and income. It is published by National Statistics and is available free on the Web at *www.statistics.gov.uk/products/p361.asp*.

Film and Television Survey

The Film and Television (FTV) Survey collects data on international trade for the film and TV sectors. In 1999, a total of 630 companies were approached to take part in the survey. The results form part of the balance of payments calculations and specific results are included in the annual publication *United Kingdom Trade in Services*.

Financial Statistics

Financial Statistics is a monthly digest of the key financial and monetary statistics published by National Statistics.

Financial Statistics Explanatory Handbook

Published annually by National Statistics, the *Financial Statistics Explanatory Handbook* provides detailed information on the definitions and methodologies used in compiling UK financial statistics. A free file is available on the Web at *www.statistics.gov.uk/products/p4861.asp*.

Financial Statistics Users' Group

The Financial Statistics Users' Group (FSUG) is a forum for users of official financial data.

First Releases

First Releases are published by National Statistics and give the most up-to-date information covering the key economic and business indicators. The releases usually only show selected data with a brief commentary and the data may be revised in subsequent publications. The releases are free on the Web at URL: *www.statistics.gov.uk/ press_releases/CurrentReleases.asp.*

Food and Agricultural Organisation

The Food and Agricultural Organisation (FAO) is a United Nations body which compiles and publishes various statistics on agriculture, land use, forestry, fishing, and food. Free access to many of the statistics is available on the FAO Web site at:

www.apps.fao.org/page/collections?subset=agriculture

www.apps.fao.org/page/collections?subset=fisheries

www.apps.fao.org/page/collections?subset=forestry

Forecast of the UK Economy

The *Forecast of the UK Economy* is published monthly by HM Treasury and provides a summary of key forecasts from the UK's leading forecasting organisations. Recent issues can be downloaded from *www.hm-treasury.gov.uk/Economic_Data_and_Tools/Forecast_for_the_UK_ Economy/data_forecasts-index.cfm?*

Gender Statistics Users' Group

The Gender Statistics Users' Group provides a forum for users of official statistics relating to gender issues.

General Household Survey

The General Household Survey (GHS) is a continuous survey of around 12,000 households in Great Britain. The sample frame is based on the Postcode Address File and all adults in the household are included in the survey. Established in 1971, its aim is to obtain a range of information on households and household characteristics, social groups, and social indicators. Questions on major topics such as housing, migration, employment, education, health, and family characteristics are asked each year; other questions may only be asked occasionally. For example, questions on drinking habits, leisure activities, and share ownership have been asked in specific years.

The annual report of the GHS is *Living in Britain* published by National Statistics and the 1998 report is available free on the Web at *www.statistics.gov.uk/products/p5756.asp.*

Government Statistical Service

The Government Statistical Service (GSS) is the collective name given to all the statistical activities carried out by central government and its departments in the UK.

GSS Methodology Series

The GSS Methodology Series is a series of monographs explaining specific methodologies used in official statistics. For example, there are monographs on GDP calculation and the background to seasonal adjustment. Available in hard copy or via the Web site at *www.statistics.gov.uk/methods_quality/publications.asp.*

Guide to Official Statistics

The *Guide to Official Statistics* provides detailed information about official statistics sources, publications, and services broken down by subject area. The latest hard copy guide is 2000 but it is also accessible free of charge on the StatBase Web pages at *www.statistics.gov.uk/products/p1551.asp.*

Guide to the Classification of Overseas Trade Statistics

The *Guide to the Classification of Overseas Trade Statistics* is an annual guide to the product headings and codes used in UK overseas trade statistics publications.

Handbook of Statistics

The *Handbook of Statistics* is a CD-ROM featuring a collection of data relevant to world trade and investment. It is published annually by the United Nations.

Health and Personal Social Services Statistics

Health and Personal Social Services Statistics is an annual publication for England and Wales with data on patients, illnesses, treatments, hospitals, etc. It is now available free on the Web at *www.doh.gov.uk/HPSSS/INDEX.HTM*

Health Statistics Quarterly

Health Statistics Quarterly provides quarterly data on health trends. It is available free on the Web at *www.statistics.gov.uk/products/p6725.asp*.

Health Statistics User Group

The Health Statistics User Group (HSUG) provides a forum for users of official health data.

Health Survey for England

The Health Survey for England (HSE) is a continuous survey of adults and children aged 2 years or over in households, undertaken by the Department of Health and based on a sample of 12,250 addresses in England. The sampling frame is the Postcode Address File. Each year, the survey covers certain key health indicators such as blood pressure, height and weight, smoking, drinking, and general health and there are specific topics investigated each year. It is published annually as the *Health Survey for England*, and data sets are on the Department of Health Web site at *www.doh.gov.uk/public/summary.htm*.

Higher Education Statistics Agency

The Higher Education Statistics Agency (HESA) is the organisation responsible for higher education statistics in the UK. Summary statistics are available at *www.hesa.ac.uk*.

Horizons

Horizons is a free quarterly newsletter from National Statistics with up-to-date information on new initiatives, surveys, and products. It is available on the Web at *www.statistics.gov.uk/newsletters.asp*.

Housing and Construction Statistics

Quarterly and annual volumes of *Housing and Construction Statistics* are produced with data covering housing and construction. A PDF file of annual statistics is downloadable free at *www.dti.gov.uk/construction/ stats/stats2001/pdf/constat2001.pdf*.

How Exactly Is Employment Measured?

How Exactly Is Employment Measured? is a booklet from National Statistics, explaining the relationship between the different sources of employment data.

Indicators of Industrial Activity

Indicators of Industrial Activity is a quarterly publication from the OECD providing a review of short-term trends in different industries in OECD countries plus total OECD, OECD – Europe, European Union, North America, G7.

Industrial Commodity Statistics Yearbook

Published annually by the United Nations, *The Industrial Commodity Statistics Yearbook* has production data for 530 commodities and products in various countries.

Inland Revenue Statistics

Inland Revenue Statistics is an annual title published by the Inland Revenue, with information and analyses on various taxes plus details of income and wealth.

Input–Output Tables for the UK

Input–output tables for the UK are published every five years by National Statistics. The latest edition (published at the end of 2000) covers 1995. These tables describe the relationships between different sectors in the economy.

The first official input–output tables for the UK were published in 1961 and covered the year 1954. Further tables, initially based on inquiries into purchases of materials and fuels by manufacturing sectors and later also service sectors, have been published for 1963, 1968, 1974, 1979, 1984, and 1990.

International Country Risk Guide

Published by Political Risk Services (PRS) Group (*www.prsgroup.com*), the monthly *International Country Risk Guide* (ICRG) collects information on 22 components of risk, groups it into three major categories (political, financial, and economic) and converts it into a single numerical risk assessment rating.

International Energy Agency

An autonomous body within the Organisation for Economic Cooperation and Development, the International Energy Agency (IEA) compiles and publishes international energy statistics. Key World Energy Statistics and other statistics are available free on the Web site at *www.iea.org/statist/index.htm*.

International Financial Statistics

International Financial Statistics (IFS) is a monthly statistical publication from the International Monetary Fund (IMF) with a range of indicators on international and domestic finance. There are detailed tables for each member country.

International Labour Organisation

The International Labour Organisation (ILO) collects and publishes international statistics on the labour market. Free access to many of the ILO statistics is available at *www.ilo.org/public/english/bureau/stat/*.

International Passenger Survey

The International Passenger Survey (IPS) is a continuous survey of passengers at UK ports and airports and through the Channel Tunnel. Based on a sample of approximately 263,000 travellers, survey indicators include country of visit (for UK residents), country of origin (for UK visitors), purpose of visit, length of stay, expenditure, mode of transport, gender, and UK regions visited. *Travel Trends* (see *Travel Trends*) is an annual report with basic results from the IPS.

International Trade in Services Survey

The International Trade in Services (ITIS) Survey was introduced in 1996 to meet the demand for improved product data on UK trade in services, and to comply with the new IMF classification of balance of payments. The ITIS Survey consists of a quarterly survey of the largest service businesses, and over 10,000 companies were contacted in survey year 1999. Data is used in the balance of payments calculations and published results from the survey appear in *United Kingdom Trade in Services*.

International Trade Statistics

International Trade Statistics is an annual statistical volume published by the World Trade Organisation (WTO), which includes a review of the latest year and an outlook for the coming year. The latest edition can be downloaded free from the Web site at *www.wto.org/english/res_e/statis_e/its2001*.

International Trade Statistics Users' Group

The International Trade Statistics Users' Group (INTRASTAT/ITSUG) provides a forum for users of international trade statistics.

Joint Industry Committee for Population Standards

Established in 1994, the Joint Industry Committee for Population Standards (JICPOPS) was set up to address the significant anomalies in population and household data being used in various advertising and market research. In 2000, JICPOPS published a set of population figures in an attempt to remove these anomalies.

Joint Industry Committee for Regional Press Research

The Joint Industry Committee for Regional Press Research (JICREG) is the single body responsible for the production of readership data for regional and local newspapers. See *www.JICREG.co.uk*.

Key Population and Vital Statistics

National and local population statistics (local authority and health authority areas) in the UK are published annually by National Statistics in *Key Population and Vital Statistics*. Available free on the Web at *www.statistics.gov.uk/products/p539.asp*.

LABORSTA

LABORSTA is a database of international labour market statistics available on the Web site of the International Labour Organisation (ILO). The database has a range of historical labour market series for various countries and there is free access to the data, along with free downloads. See *www.ilo.org/public/english/bureau/stat*.

Labour Force Statistics

Labour Force Statistics is an annual publication from the Organisation for Economic Cooperation and Development (OECD) providing data for each member country, total OECD, Euro Zone, and EU-15. The *Quarterly Labour Force Statistics* provides more up-to-date trends.

Labour Force Survey

The Labour Force Survey (LFS), a continuous survey of households in the UK, is the major source of labour market data in the UK. Similar harmonised surveys are undertaken in other EU countries, using International Labour Organisation (ILO) definitions, and Eurostat publishes aggregated results for the EU. The LFS was carried out every two years from 1973 to 1983 and annually from 1984 to 1991. The survey has been produced continually since spring 1992 in Great Britain, and winter 1994/95 in Northern Ireland.

The sampling frame is the Postcode Address File and the sample covers approximately 61,000 households in any three-month period. All adults in each household are included in the survey, which means that a sample of approximately 120,000 people is interviewed in each three-month period.

The main published output from the LFS is the *Labour Force Survey Quarterly Supplement* (see next entry). There is also an annual report and monthly releases. Online access to data is via the LFS Data service contactable at *lfs.dataservice@ons.gov.uk*.

Labour Force Survey Quarterly Supplement

The *Labour Force Survey Quarterly Supplement*, published by National Statistics, contains detailed results from the Labour Force Survey (LFS) (see above).

Labour Force Survey Results

The *Labour Force Survey Results* are annual survey results from the European Labour Force Survey undertaken by Eurostat, the Statistical Office of the European Communities.

Labour Force Survey User Guides

The *Labour Force Survey User Guides* are a 10-volume guide to Labour Force Survey (LFS) data from National Statistics. There is free access to the user guides on the Web at *www.statistics.gov.uk/products/p1537.asp*.

Labour Market Statistics Users' Group

The Labour Market Statistics Users' Group (LMSUG) provides a forum for users of official labour market statistics.

Labour Market Trends

Labour Market Trends is a monthly journal from National Statistics with articles and all the key official statistics on the labour market. There is free access to latest issues on the Web at *www.statistics.gov/products/p550.asp*.

Learning and Training at Work

Learning and Training at Work (LATW) is a new multi-purpose survey of employers that investigates the provision of learning and training at work. This information was previously collected in the Skill Needs in Britain (SNIB) surveys. The LATW 1999 survey consisted of 4,008 telephone interviews with employers having one or more employees.

Living in Britain

Living in Britain, published by National Statistics, is the annual report of the General Household Survey (GHS) with data on household characteristics, lifestyles, and other socio-economic data. The 1998 annual report is available free on the Web at *www.statistics.gov/products/p5756.asp*.

Local Housing Statistics

The *Local Housing Statistics* are quarterly statistics for local authorities in England covering the progress of house building, house renovation, sale of housing land and housing by local authorities, and other local housing data. There is free access to housing statistics on the Web at *www.housing.detr.gov.uk/research/hss/hs2000/index.htm*.

Long Range World Population Projections

Published every two years by the United Nations, the population projections are for world, regions, and countries and cover a projected 50-year period, with data for the last 50 years.

Longitudinal Study

The Longitudinal Study (LS) from National Statistics is a representative 1% sample of the population of England and Wales containing linked population census and vital events data. The LS began in the early 1970s by selecting everyone born on one of four specific days who was enumerated at the 1971 Census. Subsequent samples have been taken and linked from the 1981 and 1991 Censuses. The survey is continuous and there is regularly collected data on mortality, fertility, cancer registration, migration, infant mortality, etc. Various reports are published from the survey.

Main Economic Indicators

Main Economic Indicators is a monthly title providing key indicators for the 29 member countries of the Organisation for Economic Cooperation and Development (OECD). From March 2000, it has also included data on 10 non-member countries.

Main Science And Technology Indicators

Main Science and Technology Indicators is published annually by OECD and is a leading international source of R&D expenditure and resources data.

Manchester Information & Associated Services (MIMAS)

MIMAS is a JISC-supported national data centre providing the UK higher, further education, and research community with online access to key data and information resources. Sources include the Population Census, macro-economic data, and National Statistics data. At *www.mimas.ac.uk.*

Manufacturing Industry Surveys

Manufacturing Industry Surveys are carried out monthly and quarterly in 15 EU member countries using a standard methodology. The surveys are used to elicit opinions on production, order book, export, stocks, price, employment, capacity utilization, and competitive position expectations. The results are published in *European Economy Series B – Business and Consumer Survey Results* from the Office for Official Publications of the European Communities.

Mid-200- Population Estimates for England and Wales

The *Mid-200- Population Estimates* are annual mid-year population estimates for the UK and constituent countries, plus sub-national estimates for England and Wales, published by National Statistics. There are similar publications for Scotland and Northern Ireland. The latest estimates are available free on the Web at *www.statistics.gov.uk/products/p601.asp.*

Monthly Digest of Statistics

Published by National Statistics, the *Monthly Digest of Statistics* is a monthly compilation of key economic, business, demographic and social statistics. Recent issues are available free on the Web at *www.statistics.gov.uk/products/p611.asp.*

Monthly Review of External Trade

The *Monthly Review of External Trade* is a monthly monitor of trends in UK overseas trade. The print version was stopped in 2001 and issues are now available free on the Web at *www.statistics.gov.uk/products/p613.asp*.

Motor Trade Inquiry

The *Motor Trade Inquiry* is a sample survey by National Statistics covering approximately 6,000 businesses. First held in 1950, the survey has covered the UK since 1996 and the results are usually published within 18 months of the survey year in *Sector Review: Motor Trades*.

National Accounts of OECD Countries

Volume I of the *National Accounts of OECD Countries* covers the main aggregates of the national accounts of member countries; Volume II details the disaggregated accounts. The OECD also publishes *Quarterly National Accounts*, summarising trends in 23 OECD countries plus OECD in total, OECD-Europe, the European Union, Euro Zone, and G7.

National Accounts Users' Group

The National Accounts Users' Group (NAUG) provides a forum for users of official national accounts data.

National Centre for Social Research

The National Centre for Social Research publishes regular surveys of social attitudes and opinions and advises official statisticians on content and methodologies for official surveys. See *www.natcen.ac.uk*.

National Diet and Nutrition Survey

The National Diet and Nutrition Survey (NDNS) is a regular survey from the Department of Health.

National Digital Archive of Datasets (NDAD)

National Digital Archive of Datasets (NDAD) offers open access to archived statistics from Government departments. Free access after registration at *www.ndad.ulcc.ac.uk*.

National Food Survey

The National Food Survey (NFS) provides information on the consumption of, and expenditure on, food and food items (including eating out) by households, and nutritional intake from food eaten. Established in

1940, and in its present form in 1952, the survey was conducted by the Ministry of Agriculture Fisheries & Food (MAFF) up to 2001. The department was then replaced by the Department of Environment, Food and Rural Affairs (DEFRA). It is a continuous survey of over 10,000 households in the UK and the survey respondent is the person responsible for domestic food arrangements. Households take part voluntarily in the survey for one week. The sampling frame is the Postcode Address File in Great Britain and the Valuation and Lands Agency Property in Northern Ireland.

An annual report, the *National Food Survey*, is published some months after the survey year with detailed data by food categories and food products. A quarterly press release provides more up-to-date data for key food categories. This can be downloaded from the DEFRA Web site at *www.defra.gov.uk/esg/work_htm/Index/food.htm*.

Data on specific food items can be supplied by DEFRA for a fee.

From April 2001, the data collection and validation phases of the NFS merged with the Family Expenditure Survey (see Family Expenditure Survey). The new survey – Expenditure and Food Survey (EFS) – (see that entry) will still publish results for food and drink separately.

National Online Manpower Information Service

The National Online Manpower Information Service (NOMIS) is a database of labour market statistics operated by the University of Durham on behalf of National Statistics. The database covers a range of labour market data particularly at sub-national level: unemployment, employment, earnings, vacancies, training, plus demographic and population census data. From Summer 2001, NOMIS has been offering free Web access to data in line with other government produced statistics. See *www.nomisweb.co.uk*.

National Readership Survey

The National Readership Survey (NRS), from National Readership Surveys Ltd, is a continuous survey of 38,000 adults aged 15 and over in Great Britain. The sampling frame is the Postcode Address File. The survey examines the readership of national newspapers and various consumer magazines and results are analysed by various demographic characteristics, such as age, sex, social class, region, etc. Full results are available to clients and headline results are on the NRS Web site at *www.nrs.co.uk*.

National Statistics

Established in 2000, National Statistics is the new identity for UK government statistics. The National Statistics logo will appear only on statistics which meet rigorous standards of data collection, processing, and dissemination. These are set out in a new National Statistics code of practice. See also Statistics.gov.uk.

National Statistics DataBank

The National Statistics DataBank holds economic and financial time series in electronic format, and these time series correspond to the major series found in the core economic and financial official statistical publications. Over 55,000 time series are covered and access is via a subscription. The data can be supplied via the Web, disk, or hard copy but the DataBank is designed for use by heavy users, such as institutional users. Individual users are likely to find StatBase more relevant (see that entry).

Individual time series in the DataBank are each given a four-letter code and these codes are also published in the relevant tables in hard copy publications from National Statistics (see National Statistics DataBank Codes in chapter 1).

As this guide was going to press, it was announced that DataBank had been merged with another database, TimeZone, to form a new free Web service called Time Series Data, accessible via main *www.statistics.gov* web site.

National Statistics First Releases

National Statistics First Releases are a series of statistical press releases produced at regular intervals (monthly, quarterly, annually) on key economic, financial, and business trends. They are available free on the Web at *www.statistics.gov.uk/press_releases/CurrentReleases.asp*.

National Statistics Information and Library Service

The National Statistics Information and Library Service (NSILS) is based around two major collections of statistical data and other information, one based in London and one in Newport. The London site has holdings of social statistics, business and economic data, statistical series from other government departments, and some international sources. The Newport office has more extensive economic and business collections and some non-governmental sources such as trade associations and market research reports. Both sites can be visited and there are telephone and email enquiry facilities:

*   Office for National Statistics Library, 1 Drummond Gate, Pimlico, London SW1V 2QQ

- Office for National Statistics Library, Government Buildings, Cardiff Road, Newport, South Wales NP10 8XG.
- telephone enquiries: 020 7533 5888
- email: *info@statistics.gov.uk*.

National Statistics Omnibus Survey

The National Statistics Omnibus Survey is a continuous survey commissioned by National Statistics and involving around 1,900 adults in each survey month. The survey, established in October 1990, is conducted in Great Britain and the results are available nationally and at standard region level. Results are available within four weeks of the survey completion.

National Statistics Online Services

The National Statistics Online Services Branch provides details of all online services. For further information, contact:

- Online Services Branch, B1/12, 1 Drummond Gate, London SW1V 2QQ
- telephone enquiries: 020 7533 5675
- email: *on-line.services.branch@statistics.gov.uk*.

National Travel Survey

The National Travel Survey (NTS) is a continuous survey of over 3,000 households per year in Great Britain, established in 1988. The survey is the responsibility of the Department of Transport, Local Government and the Regions. The sampling frame is the Postcode Address File.

Neighbourhood Statistics Service

Launched in 2001, Neighbourhood Statistics Service provides small area statistics from National Statistics available for regions, counties, local government areas, and postcode areas. Access to the service is via the UK government statistics Web site at *www.statistics.gov.uk/neighbourhood/home.asp*.

New Cronos

New Cronos is Eurostat's database for macroeconomic and social statistics. Economic time series are published from this database and Eurostat Data Shops can answer inquiries regarding economic data from New

Cronos. Further information is available at URL: *www.datashop.org/en/ newcronos.html*.

New Earnings Survey

The New Earnings Survey (NES) is an annual survey based on employee records held by employers in Great Britain. Employers supply data on a 1% sample of employees who are members of PAYE schemes. For the 1999 sample, approximately 223,000 were selected and there was a 89.9% response rate. Data collected includes gross weekly and hourly earnings and hours worked with an analysis by occupation, industry, age, sex, region, and country, plus small area data, collective agreements, manual/ non-manual workers, full-time and part-time status. The results also show the make-up of pay, overtime hours worked, and public/private sector earnings.

The results are published annually in various volumes by National Statistics under the general title *New Earnings Survey*. New Earnings Survey – GB (Parts A–F) offer various analyses and *New Earnings Survey UK Volume* is a summary volume.

Full results are available free on the Web in various files:

Part A – 	*www.statistics.gov.uk/products/p5749.asp*.
Part B – 	*www.statistics.gov.uk/products/p5750.asp*.
Part C – 	*www.statistics.gov.uk/products/p5751.asp*.
Part D – 	*www.statistics.gov.uk/products/p5752.asp*.
Part E – 	*www.statistics.gov.uk/products/p5753.asp*.
Part F – 	*www.statistics.gov.uk/products/p5754.asp*.
UK Volume – 	*www.statistics.gov.uk/p647.asp*.

NOMIS

See National Online Manpower Information Service.

OECD

OECD is the Organisation for Economic Co-operation and Development (see that entry), a leading producer of international statistics.

OECD Economic Outlook

Published twice a year, *OECD Economic Outlook* offers commentary and data on short-term economic trends in member countries and major non-OECD economies.

OECD Employment Outlook

OECD Employment Outlook is an annual analysis of labour market issues accompanied by key labour market statistics.

OECD Historical Statistics

OECD Historical Statistics is an annual publication with economic indicators for over a 30-year period.

OECD in Figures

OECD in Figures is an annual publication containing key data on OECD countries.

OECD STAN Database for Industrial Analysis

The *OECD STAN Database for Industrial Analysis* contains annual data on 49 manufacturing sectors in 22 OECD countries with data for the latest 10 years. The data is taken from STructural ANalysis Industrial Database (STAN).

Office for National Statistics

The Office for National Statistics (ONS) is the co-ordinating body for official statistics in the UK.

Organisation for Economic Co-Operation and Development

The Organisation for Economic Co-operation and Development (OECD) is a leading producer of international economic, business and social statistics. It has 29 member countries which are covered by these statistics: Australia, Austria, Belgium, Canada, Czech Republic, Denmark, Finland, France, Germany, Greece, Hungary, Iceland, Ireland, Italy, Japan, Korea, Luxembourg, Mexico, Netherlands, New Zealand, Norway, Poland, Portugal, Spain, Sweden, Switzerland, Turkey, UK, and USA. Increasingly, the OECD also collects statistics from non-member countries such as Russia, China, and Brazil.

Overseas Trade Statistics

Overseas Trade Statistics are published regularly in various volumes, most of which have specific product data as well as general trends. The main volumes include:

- *Overseas Trade Statistics* (OTSA) – an annual publication with details of UK trade with the EU and the rest of the world
- *Overseas Trade Statistics* (OTSG) – a guide to the classification used for overseas trade statistics; it provides a detailed breakdown of the Standard International Trade Classification (SITC) and its correlation with the Combined Nomenclature (CN)
- *Overseas Trade Statistics* (OTS1) – a monthly volume covering UK trade, at product level, with countries outside the EU
- *Overseas Trade Statistics* (OTS2) – a monthly volume covering UK trade with the EU
- *Overseas Trade Statistics* (OTSQ) – a quarterly report on UK trade with the EU
- General trends in overseas trade are monitored monthly in the *Monthly Review of External Trade* (see that entry). Detailed trade data is available at *www.uktradeinfo.com*.

PACSTAT Production and Construction Statistics

The *PACSTAT Production and Construction Statistics* is an annual CD-ROM from National Statistics allowing for the manipulation of production and construction data taken from the Annual Business Inquiry (ABI) and other sources.

Partnership in Statistics for Development

The Partnership in Statistics for Development in the 21st Century (Paris21) is a consortium of 90 countries and international statistical agencies that have come together to raise awareness of the value of good statistics.

Pink Book

The Pink Book is the popular name for the annual United Kingdom Balance of Payments publication (see *UK Balance of Payments – the Pink Book*).

Population Census Reports

Various reports are published offering results from the population census (see that entry in chapter 3) and there are also other services available offering more detailed and customised analysis of census data.

Usually, the first detailed results from the UK population census are published in a series of *County Monitors* (England and Wales) and *Re-*

gional Monitors (Scotland), which are short pamphlets for each area with key results. These are followed by *County Reports* and *Regional Reports*, which are more substantial reports for each area with detailed results. *National Report: Great Britain* brings together the main variables included in the above reports and there are similar publications for Scotland, Wales, and Northern Ireland. From the 1991 census, there were also reports for specific local authority areas.

Census reports are published on specific topics, with national and local data, and topic reports from the 1991 census include: ethnic group and country of birth; long-term illness; sex, age and marital status; migration; workplace and transport to work; housing; household composition; communal establishments; economic activity; and qualified manpower.

Information on the progress of the 2001 Census, including details of any results, can be found at *www.statistics.gov.uk/census2001/default.asp*. Details of how to access results from previous censuses can be found at *www.statistics.gov.uk/census2001/accesscensus.asp*.

Population Trends

Population Trends is a quarterly publication bringing together the main demographic statistics, plus features on population issues. It is published by National Statistics, and recent issues are available free on the Web at *www.statistics.gov.uk/products/p6303.asp*.

Poster Advertising Research

Poster Advertising Research (POSTAR) provides data on the awareness and frequency of visits relating to outdoor poster advertising.

Price Adjustment Formulae – Monthly Bulletin Of Indices

Price Adjustment Formulae – Monthly Bulletin of Indices contains monthly price indices for labour and work done in the UK construction sector. It is published by the Department of Industry (DTI). There is free access to the data on the Web at *www.dti.gov.uk/construction/stats/indices.htm*.

Price Index Numbers for Current Cost Accounting

The *Price Index Numbers for Current Cost Accounting* are published monthly and contain detailed indices for the revaluation of assets and stocks, providing a guide to capital replacement costs. Recent issues are available free on the Web at *www.statistics.gov.uk/products/p2206.asp*.

PRODCOM Industry Reports

The *PRODCOM Industry Reports*, previously called Product Sales and Trade Reports, are a series of reports for specific industries based on data derived from the PRODCOM Inquiry (see next entry). There are 91 annual reports covering 203 industries, and 33 quarterly reports for 47 industries. All the reports are available free on the Web at *www.statistics.gov.uk/products/p611.asp*.

PRODCOM Inquiry

The PRODCOM Inquiry from National Statistics provides data on the value and volume of UK manufacturer's product sales. PRODCOM (PRODucts of the European COMmunity) is a harmonised system used in EU countries for the collection and publication of product statistics (see PRODCOM in chapter 1). The PRODCOM Inquiry consists of a quarterly and an annual survey with 25,000 businesses surveyed annually and 4,500 businesses surveyed quarterly. PRODCOM data can be matched with product import and export data from HM Customs and Excise and this latter data is published alongside the PRODCOM data in Prodcom Industry Reports (see previous entry). These report series offer individual reports for specific product sectors. There are 91 annual volumes covering 203 industries, and 33 quarterly volumes for 47 industries.

PRODCOM List

The *PRODCOM List* is published annually by Eurostat and is a list of all the sectors and products, with their relevant codes, covered by PRODCOM.

Production and Construction Inquiries – Summary Volume

The *Production and Construction Inquiries – Summary Volume* is an annual volume, published by National Statistics, based on the results of the Annual Business Inquiry (ABI) and containing data at the two-, three-, and five-digit levels of the Standard Industrial Classification (SIC). It gives a general indication of the performance of specific industry sectors.

Public Expenditure Statistical Analyses

The *Public Expenditure Statistical Analyses* are published annually by the Treasury with data on public sector spending.

Radio Joint Audience Research

Established in 1992, Radio Joint Audience Research (RAJAR) provides a single measurement system for radio audiences, including both the BBC and commercial radio. Summary data are available on the Web at *www.rajar.co.uk*

Regio

Regio is Eurostat's database of regional statistics from which statistical products such as regional statistics are produced. Eurostat Data Shops can answer inquiries on regional data from Regio.

Regional Trends

Regional Trends is an annual publication from National Statistics providing economic, business, demographic, and social indicators for UK regions and local authority areas. There are also comparisons with other regions in the UK. Recent issues are available free on the Web at *www.statistics.gov.uk/products/p836.asp*.

Regions Statistical Yearbook

The *Regions Statistical Yearbook* is an annual publication from Eurostat with statistics for Nomenclature of Territorial Units for Statistics (NUTS) regions in the European Union.

Residential Property Price Report

The *Residential Property Price Report* is a quarterly free report on the average prices of residential property and sales volume in the UK by region and local authority area. It is produced by HM Land Registry and is available free on the Web at *www.landreg.gov.uk/ppr/*.

Resource Centre for Access to Data on Europe

Based at the University of Durham, the Resource Centre for Access to Data on Europe (rcade) provides access to Eurostat statistics free to academics; access is available to others for a fee. At the end of 2000, rcade announced that it was reducing the services it was able to offer on its Web site at *www.-rcade.dur.ac.uk*.

Retail Prices Index Technical Manual

The *Retail Prices Index Technical Manual* is an ad-hoc publication from National Statistics explaining the definitions and methodologies used in the compilation of the retail prices index (RPI) (see chapter 2).

Retail Sales

The monthly *Retail Sales* contains results from the Retail Sales Inquiry, published by National Statistics. There is free access to the data on the Web at *www.statistics.gov.uk/products/p1478.asp.*

Retail Sales Inquiry

The Retail Sales Inquiry is a monthly survey of retail sales from National Statistics based on a sample survey of 5,000 retail businesses in Great Britain. The survey includes all large retailers and a representative panel of smaller retailers. Data from the inquiry is published in the monthly Retail Sales (see entry above) and the monthly *Service Sector: Retail Sales.*

Retail Trade Surveys

The Retail Trade Surveys are carried out monthly and quarterly in 14 EU member countries using a standard methodology. The surveys elicit opinions on sales, stocks, orders with suppliers, employment expectations. The results are published in *European Economy Series B – Business and Consumer Survey Results* from the Office for Official Publications of the European Communities.

Retailing Inquiry

The annual Retailing Inquiry Survey is undertaken by National Statistics for 10,000 businesses in the UK. It contains data on turnover, employees, stocks, purchases, capital expenditure, outlets, commodity sales, etc. There have been annual inquiries since 1976, with results usually published within 18 months of the survey year in *Sector Review: Retailing.*

Sector Reviews – Manufacturing

Published by National Statistics, individual sector reviews provide data on the structure of, and trends in, specific industries. Regular quarterly titles include food, drink and tobacco; textiles; clothing, footwear and leather goods; and chemicals. Titles covering other sectors are produced on an ad-hoc basis.

Sector Reviews – Services

Published by National Statistics, there are individual sector reviews providing data on the structure of, and trends in, specific service sectors. Titles include: motor trades; catering and allied trades; retailing; wholesaling; and service trades.

Service Trades Inquiry

The annual Service Trades Inquiry is a sample survey carried out by National Statistics covering approximately 18,800 businesses. Originally developed in the 1950s, it was run annually until 1979 when it became biennial. Since 1986, it has been annual again. More service sectors have been added to the inquiry in recent years. The results are usually published within 18 months of the survey year in *Sector Review: Service Trades*.

Size Analysis of UK Businesses

Using data taken from the Inter-departmental Business Register, the annual volume Size Analysis of UK Businesses describes UK VAT-registered enterprises by turnover, employment, legal status, VAT trade classification, region, county, and local authority district. It is published by National Statistics, and there is free access to recent volumes on the web at *www.statistics.gov.uk/products/p933.asp*.

Social Focus Series

The Social Focus Series is a series of short reports from National Statistics containing analysis and data on specific social groups. Titles published include:

- Social Focus on Children
- Social Focus on Ethnic Minorities
- Social Focus on Families
- Social Focus on Men
- Social Focus on Older People
- Social Focus on the Unemployed
- Social Focus on Women
- Social Focus on Women and Men
- Social Focus on Young People.

Social Situation in the European Union

The first edition of *Social Situation in the European Union* was published in 2000.

Social Trends

Social Trends is an annual compilation of social and economic data which aims to describe British society and changes over the years. Tables and graphs are accompanied by easy-to-understand commentary. It is published by National Statistics, and there is free access to recent issues on the Web at *www.statistics.gov.uk/products/p5748.asp*.

SourceOECD

SourceOECD is an online database of OECD publications and statistics. The online statistics service was launched in 2000. See *www.sourceoecd.org*.

StatBase

StatBase is the database of National Statistics which is freely available on the UK government statistics Web site. The database contains detailed descriptions of all the official data sources, descriptions of publications and services, and access to selected time series and indicators. There are four elements to the database:

- Statsearch – provides details of the types of statistics available, publications and services, and the datasets on the database. This section can be searched at three levels: themes (e.g. education, economy): subjects within themes (e.g. primary schools, prices); topics within subjects (e.g. pupil numbers, producer prices).

- Statstore – contains the actual datasets referred to in Statsearch. These can be accessed from an alphabetical list or through a search at two levels: theme (e.g. education); and subject (primary schools). Datasets can be viewed on the screen or downloaded and all datasets are free.

- Timezone – contains more detailed economic and socio-economic data, but users require a knowledge of the various four character codes used to identify different time series (see National Statistics DataBank Codes in chapter 1).

- Textsearch – allows the user to enter a string of text and then undertake a search to identify relevant records in StatBase.

Details of, and access to, StatBase, can be found at *www.statistics.gov.uk/ statbase/mainmenu.asp*. As this guide was going to press, a new service, Times Series Data, was announced. Access is from the above URL.

Statistics Commission

Established in 2000 alongside the new National Statistics identity in the UK, the Statistics Commission is an independent, non-executive body which will publicly advise ministers on statistical integrity and quality, and will seek opinions from statistical users and providers.

Statistics.gov.uk

Statistics.gov.uk is the Web site for UK official statistics, and the gateway to statistical sources, metadata, and databases including StatBase (see that entry). UK official statistics are divided into 12 subject-specific themes and each subject theme is accessible via the site. The themes are:

- agriculture, forestry, and fishing
- commerce, energy, and industry
- compendia and reference
- crime and justice
- economy
- education and training
- health and care
- labour market
- natural and built environment
- population and migration
- social and welfare
- transport, travel and tourism.

Many official statistics in the above themes are now available free on the site, or via links to relevant departments, as well as statistical compilations such as the *Monthly Digest of Statistics, Social Trends, and Regional Trends*. The Virtual Bookshelf pages on the site have links to all publications available free on the Web.

Statistics Users' Council

The Statistics Users' Council (SUC) provides a forum for users of official statistics.

Stockbuilding

Stockbuilding is a quarterly survey of inventories (stocks) and work in progress from National Statistics.

Survey of English Housing

The *Survey of English Housing* is a continuous survey using a sample of 20,800 addresses from the Postcode Address File of households in England. Operated by the Department of Transport, Local Government and the Regions (DTLR), the survey examines households and their housing with a special focus on the private rented sector. It was first produced in 1993.

Survey of Personal Incomes

The Survey of Personal Incomes is based on income tax records at the Inland Revenue and uses a sample of approximately 125,000 cases. The data is published in annual *Inland Revenue Statistics*.

Target Group Index

The Target Group Index (TGI), produced annually by the British Market Research Bureau (BMRB), is a national product and media survey based on information supplied by 24,000 adults, who are asked to complete a detailed questionnaire in their homes. The main emphasis of the TGI is on products, brands, services, leisure, and media and it is an important source of data on the use of the above by consumers broken down by sex, age, social class, region, and media usage. Its product data measures heavy to light usage for over 4,000 brands in over 300 fast-moving consumer goods (FMCG) fields.

TGI clients include all the major media companies, advertising agencies, and many FMCG companies. The detailed results are published in 34 separate volumes: the first two volumes provide general demographic information and volumes 3–34 cover individual consumer product areas. There are detailed consumer profiles and consumer penetration figures (see Profile and Penetration in chapter 5) for each product. Survey results are expensive, with each volume priced at over £4,000, although specific data sets can be purchased.

In recent years, spin-offs have been developed from the main TGI survey. These include Premier: The Upmarket TGI, and Youth TGI. See *www.bmrb.co.uk*.

Tariff and Statistical Office

The Tariff and Statistical Office is an executive unit within HM Customs and Excise responsible for overseas trade statistics.

Time Use Survey

A Time Use Survey has been commissioned by National Statistics at regular intervals. The latest survey has run from June 2000 to July 2001 and is based on a sample of 11,000 households. The households have to keep two diaries describing their activities and time use. Previous surveys were undertaken in 1995 and 1999.

Trade Analysis and Information System

The Trade Analysis and Information System (TRAIN) is a database of international trade and tariff statistics developed by the United Nations Conference on Trade and Development (see that entry). It is based on the Harmonised Commodity Description and Coding System of trade (see chapter 1) and covers tariffs, para-tariffs, and non-tariff measures plus import flows by origin for over 100 countries. Available on the Web at *www.unctad.org/trains/index.htm* or as a CD-ROM.

Trade Partners UK Information Centre

Trade Partners UK Information Centre, previously known as the Export Marketing Intelligence Centre (EMIC), is part of the Department of Trade and Industry (DTI) and it offers access to a library of international statistical publications from international agencies and specific countries. Admission is free between 9.00 and 17.30 Monday to Friday.

- Trade Partners UK Information Centre, Kingsgate House, 66–74 Victoria Street, London SW1E 6SW
- tel: 020 7215 5444
- fax: 020 7215 4231
- *www.tradepartners.gov.uk*.

Tradstat

Tradstat is an online database of product import and export data which is part of the Dialog suite of databases. It has external trade data for 16

European countries, Canada, USA, Argentina, Brazil, and seven Asia Pacific countries. Various reports are available from the database. See *www.dialog.com/info/products/desktop-index.shtml*.

Transport Statistics Great Britain

Transport Statistics Great Britain is an annual compendium of statistics on transport sectors published by the Department of Transport, Local Government and the Regions (DTLR). Transport statistics are available on the Web at *www.transtat.dtlr.gov.uk*.

Transport Statistics Users' Group

The Transport Statistics Users' Group (TSUG) provides a forum for users of official transport statistics.

Travel Trends

Travel Trends is an annual report summarising the key results of the International Passenger Survey (IPS), see *www.statistics.gov.uk/statbase/ Product.asp?vlnk=1391&More=N*

UK Balance of Payments – the Pink Book

The *UK Balance of Payments* contains annual detailed estimates for the last 11 years. Also known as the Pink Book, it is published by National Statistics. The annual volume, plus updates, is now available free on the web at *www.statistics.gov.uk/products/p1140.asp*.

UK Economic Accounts

UK Economic Accounts is a quarterly volume from National Statistics bringing together data on national and financial accounts. Quarterly updates are available free on the web at *www.statistics.gov.uk/products/ p1904.asp*.

UK in Figures

UK in Figures is a pocket book of basic data on the UK published annually and available free. It is also available from the National Statistics home page at *www.statistics.gov.uk*.

UK Health Statistics

UK Health Statistics is a new compendium of health statistics which brings together in one volume data that was previously published in separate reports for the UK's constituent countries. It is available free on the web at *www.statistics.gov.uk/products/p6637.asp*.

UK National Accounts – the Blue Book

The *UK National Accounts*, also known as the Blue Book, is an annual publication from National Statistics offering detailed national accounts statistics. Recent volumes are available free on the web at *www.statistics.gov.uk/statbase/products/p1143.asp*.

UK National Accounts – Concepts, Sources and Methods

UK National Accounts – Concepts, Sources and Methods is an ad-hoc publication describing the UK national accounts. It was last published in 1998 by National Statistics and is available free on the Web at *www.statistics.gov.uk/products/p1144.asp*.

UK Service Sector

UK Service Sector is a new quarterly publication which first appeared in its present format in 2000. The publication is still in its pilot stage and a decision on its future will be made after monitoring the demand at this stage. The first issue was hard copy but the second issue is only available as a PDF file on the UK government statistics Web site, at *www.statistics.gov.uk/products/p5670.asp*.

UK Trade in Services

UK Trade in Services is an annual publication detailing the results of the International Trade in Services (ITIS) Survey. The third annual edition was published in 2001. It is available free on the Web at *www.statistics.gov.uk/products/p3343.asp*.

United Nations

The United Nations (UN), through its statistical office in New York and various agencies, publishes international economic, business, demographic, and social statistics. Details of its online statistical databases are available at *www.un.org/depts/unsd/sd_databases.htm*.

UN Conference on Trade and Development

The UN Conference on Trade and Development (UNCTAD) publishes various statistical titles on world trade. See *www.unctad.org/en/pub/ps1tdr01.en.htm*.

UN Demographic Yearbook

The *UN Demographic Yearbook* has basic demographic data for member countries and each issue also covers a specific demographic topic, e.g. migration, age structure, censuses, etc.

UN Economic Commission for Europe

The UN Economic Commission for Europe (UN/ECE) produces various economic, social, demographic and business statistics on Europe, including the countries of the former Soviet Union.

UN Industrial Development Organisation

The United Nations Industrial Development Organisation (UNIDO) is responsible for the collection and publication of general industrial statistics from the UN member countries. A separate UN statistical unit, Statistics Division of UN, is responsible for the publication of international commodity production data. See *www.unido.org/doc/50215.html*.

UN Monthly Bulletin of Statistics

The *UN Monthly Bulletin of Statistics* is a monthly statistical compilation from the United Nations with sections on population, employment, mining, manufacturing, trade, earnings, prices, and finance.

UN National Accounts Statistics: Analysis of Main Aggregates

The *UN National Accounts Statistics: Analysis of Main Aggregates* is an annual publication from the United Nations covering key national accounts variables for member countries.

UN Population and Vital Statistics Report

The *UN Population and Vital Statistics Report* is published at regular intervals and gives population estimates for the world, and its regions and countries.

UN Statistical Yearbook

The *UN Statistical Yearbook* is an annual yearbook covering over 200 countries and with 10-year time series for many indicators. The 2000 edition was the 44th edition.

UN/ECE Statistical Yearbook

The *UN/ECE Statistical Yearbook* is published annually by the UN Economic Commission for Europe (UN/ECE).

United Nations Educational, Scientific and Cultural Organisation

The United Nations Educational, Scientific and Cultural Organisation (UNESCO) publishes statistics on the above themes, including the UNESCO Statistical Yearbook (see that entry).

UNESCO Facts and Figures

UNESCO Facts and Figures presents basic data on world educational and cultural trends.

UNESCO Institute for Statistics

Established in 1999, the UNESCO Institute for Statistics aims to reform and improve the statistical capabilities of UNESCO.

UNESCO Statistical Yearbook

The *UNESCO Statistical Yearbook* is an annual international statistical title with sections covering population, education, culture, social, and leisure trends in specific countries.

World Bank

The World Bank publishes statistics on economic and social development issues through a series of publications and electronic products. There is free access to its country data on the Web at URL: *www.worldbank.org/data/countrydata/countrydata.html*; also free access to data by topic at *www.worldbank.org/databytopic/databytopic.html*.

World Bank Atlas

The *World Bank Atlas* is an annual publication from the World Bank with maps and diagrams for 210 economies. The data covers population, economy, environment, and markets.

World Development Indicators

World Development Indicators (*WDI*) is an annual publication from the World Bank with data on people, society, environment, economy, and markets in 148 countries and 15 country groupings. There is free access to country data on the Web at *www.worldbank.org/data/countrydata/ countrydata.html*.

World Education Indicators

World Education Indicators (WEI) is a system of global statistics aiming to offer standardised data across countries. A joint initiative involving UNESCO and the OECD.

World Statistics Pocketbook

World Statistics Pocketbook is an annual pocketbook of key world statistics published by the United Nations.

Yearbook of Labour Statistics

The *Yearbook of Labour Statistics* is the major international source of labour market statistics published annually by the International Labour Organisation (ILO). Covering over 190 countries, areas and territories, the tables provide data for a 10-year period. There is free access to data on the web at *www.ilo.org/public/english/bureau/stat/*.

Youth Cohort Study

The Youth Cohort Study is a biennial survey of young people aged 16–19 in England and Wales. A sample of approximately 22,500 individuals is selected from school records. The young people are surveyed in the year after their compulsory education ends to obtain information on economic activity. The department responsible is the Department for Education and Skills, *www.dfes.gov.uk/index.htm*.

7

Terminologies, concepts, and statistical devices

The terminologies, concepts, and devices used in published statistics can be confusing. This chapter considers some of these and explains their construction and use in more detail. In particular, there are detailed explanations of terms such as current and constant prices which are used in many time series, and index numbers, which are the basis of many published time series. Both explanations give examples which enable readers to construct their own indexes and calculate their own current and constant time series. Other frequently published terminologies such as provisional and revised figures, seasonally adjusted figures, net supply figures, manufacturer's selling prices, and retail selling prices are also described.

The chapter also outlines some of the core survey and statistical techniques such as sampling, and key areas of statistical analysis such as measures of central tendency, and measures of dispersion. There is only a cursory consideration of these techniques here offering an introduction to the methodological basis of many published time series. Further information on survey sampling and data analysis techniques can be obtained from the range of books and guides available on this topic.

Annual Figures

Most annual published statistics refer to the calendar year, but this is not always the case with annual data: some annual figures relate to the 12 months up to the latest month available for example (see Moving Annual Total). There are also some instances where it is more appropriate to publish annual figures in different time frames. For example, the annual crop year for fruit and vegetables in the UK runs from May to June and the published data on production of these crops uses this annual time frame. Calendar year data is also published.

Apparent Consumption

See Net Supply.

Base Year

The base year is usually the first year in a time series of index figures, with index calculations for all other years based on the change from this base year. The base year figure is usually expressed as 100, i.e. 1995 = 100. Sometimes, the base year may not be the first year in an index series but simply the year chosen to compare other years with. In this situation, there may be index figures based on the change from the base year for years before the base year as well as years after the base year. Where index series are monthly, quarterly, or weekly, the base period will also be a month, quarter, or week, i.e. January 1995 = 100, Quarter 2 1999 = 100.

Base-weighted Index

See Index Numbers.

Bear Market

A bear market for shares is a falling market (i.e. share prices are falling) where 'bears' prosper. Bears are investors who sell securities at a higher price in the hope of buying them back at a lower price.

Bellweather Survey

A bellweather survey, or bellweather data, is a survey of a specific population which can then be used to offer a guide to broader trends. For example, a survey of marketing or advertising expenditure by companies offers some guide to economic conditions and confidence as companies generally spend more on marketing and advertising if their economic position is healthy.

Bias

Bias in survey methodology is the extent to which, over repeated samples, the mean of the sampling distribution differs from the true mean, i.e. the difference between sample results and the results that would be obtained if all the population was surveyed. It is difficult to quantify bias but it is likely to increase when the response rate is very low, or the sample used in a survey is deficient in some way.

Bull Market

A bull market for shares is a rising market (i.e. share prices are increasing) where 'bulls' prosper. Bulls are investors who buy securities at a lower price in the hope of selling them at a higher price.

Chained Index

See Index Numbers.

CIF

CIF (cost of insurance and freight) is the basis of the valuation of imports for customs purposes. It includes the cost of insurance premiums and freight costs. Exports are valued in a different way (see FOB) and insurance and freight costs need to be deducted from import values to be consistent with export values.

Common Currencies

When value data is being compared across national boundaries, the data is often converted into one currency to make this comparison easier. For example, it is difficult to compare the retail markets for wines in France, Germany, UK, and the USA if the basis of each country's market value is their national currency. The user is comparing markets measured by four separate currency values. By converting all these currencies to one currency, for example the US dollar, the pound, or the French franc, it is easier to compare markets and trends.

Many international published statistics use the US dollar as the common currency. A disadvantage of using one common currency is that apparent variations in market sizes from one country to the next, and increases or decreases in this apparent market size from one time period to the next, may be due to changes in exchange rates rather than to any real changes in the market itself. Any significant changes in exchange rates between one currency and the US dollar, for example, will have a noticeable effect on any common currency calculations if the common currency used is the US dollar.

Composite Index

See Index Numbers.

Compound Annual Average Growth Rate

The Compound Annual Average Growth Rate (CAAGR) reflects the annual average growth rate for each year in a series of years from the base year to the last year. Compound growth rates mean that growth is compounded from a higher base over time. For example, if sales are increasing by 1% a month, over a 12-month period sales will not increase by 12% (or 1% ∞ 12) but 12.7%. This is because each month's sales are 1% greater than the month before and each monthly percentage increase is compounded from a higher base. So a 12.7% a year increase is the same as a 1% a month increase annualised. See also Growth Rates.

Constant Prices

Constant prices, sometimes referred to 'real' prices, are used when a product or service sold is valued on the basis of the price in some selected time period. The current price (see Current Prices) refers to the actual price of a product or service at a given time or in a given time period. When measuring trends over time, statistics based on current prices may be influenced by inflation or deflation and may not give a real picture of changes in output or volumes. Here is an example of a market measured in current prices over three years in the month of January:

Sales of chocolate cakes at current prices

	Value	% change
Year 1 – January	£100	–
Year 2 – January	£120	20.0
Year 3 – January	£126	5.0

In year 2, sales increased by an impressive 20% to £120 and, in year 3, although sales growth was less impressive, there was still growth of 5% compared with January in the previous year. However, what these figures fail to show is the effect of price changes on sales growth and this can only be taken into account when sales at constant prices are tabulated:

Sales of chocolate cakes at constant prices

	Number of cakes sold	Price of each cake	Sales at current prices	Sales at constant prices
Year 1 – January	100	£1	£100	£100
Year 2 – January	100	£1.20	£120	£100
Year 3 – January	90	£1.40	£126	£90

In year 2, sales increased by 20% at current prices to £120 but an analysis of the number of cakes sold and the price of each cake shows that although the market value increased by 20% at current prices in year 2, this was entirely due to a 20% increase in the price of each cake from £1 to £1.20. The number of cakes actually sold in year 2 stayed at 100, the same as the previous year. In year 3, sales at current prices increased by 5% over the previous year to £126, but an analysis of the number of cakes sold and the price of each cake shows that although the market value increased by 5%, the number of cakes sold actually fell to 90 but the price of each cake increased to £1.40. This increase in price helped to offset the declining number of cakes sold and led to an increase in sales of 5% at current prices.

The growth in the value of the market from year 1 to year 3 was been due to increased prices and not due to any real growth in the market. Quite the opposite – the number of cakes sold has actually fallen. Measuring sales growth at constant prices removes any price changes from the calculation and presents a real picture of growth or otherwise in a market. Trends at constant prices are calculated by taking the price that was paid for a product or service in a particular time period and then calculating subsequent sales using this original price. In our example above, the constant price calculation is based on the price of £1 in the first year. Sales at constant prices in year 2 were £100, as in the first year, because 100 cakes were sold at £1 if the inflationary element is excluded.

In year 3, only 90 cakes were sold at £1 (again removing the inflationary element) so the market value actually fell in constant price terms to £90.

In published statistics, time series in current and constant prices are often shown side-by-side. GDP figures, for example, are usually published at both current and constant prices. Tables headed 'GDP at 1995 prices' or 'GDP at 1999 prices' simply mean that the constant price calculations have used the prices prevailing in the year referred to as the base year for the time series.

Correlation

Correlation is the measure of the strength of the linear association between two variables: in other words, the measure of the degree to which changes in one variable might affect the other variable. A strong positive correlation shows that as one variable rises or falls, so does another. Negative correlation exists when one variable decreases as the other increases. Zero correlation means that no pattern is clearly discernible between the two variables.

Current Prices

Published statistical tables and time series often refer to the value of an indicator at 'current prices' (sometimes the terms 'market prices' or 'actual prices' may be used). For example, GDP at current prices, or retail sales of chocolate confectionery at current prices. The current price refers to the actual price of a product or service at a given time, or in a given time period (day, week, month, quarter, or year). Here is a theoretical example:

If 100 chocolate cakes sell at £1 each in January, then the value of the market at current prices in January is 100 ∞ £1 or £100.

When comparing trends over time, or different time periods within a statistical time series, statistics based on current prices should be used carefully since current or actual prices in any given time period may be influenced by inflation or deflation. Changes in current price data over time may simply reflect increases or decreases in prices of goods and services rather than any real changes in output or volumes. Here is a simple example:

The value of GDP at current prices in a country in a specific year may have increased by 3% but, if inflation in the same country increased by 4% over the same time period, then GDP actually fell by 1%. Simply measuring GDP growth at current prices without considering this inflation would give a misleading picture of economic growth. This is why another measure – the value of an indicator at constant prices – is often used instead of, or alongside, the current price measure. See Constant Prices for more details.

Current-Weighted Index

See Index Numbers.

Cyclical Indicators

Cyclical or leading indicators are useful aids to predicting short-term changes in economic and business activity. These indicators can help to predict turning points in the economic or business cycle (see Cyclical Variation). Indicators which turn in advance of changes of GDP, for example, can be used to predict economic changes. These are often referred to as leading indicators: business confidence, housing starts, share prices peak about 12–16 months ahead of output, consumer credit and manufacturing orders peak about six months ahead, retail sales peak about three months ahead. Lagging indicators peak after changes in GDP. For example, growth in average earnings is about four months after output changes, and investment around 12 months after.

Some countries, and international statistical agencies such as the Organisation for Economic Cooperation and Development (OECD), combine groups of economic and business indicators into composite cyclical indicators (CCIs), sometimes referred to as composite leading indicators (CLIs). Presented as a index, these series remove trends and erratic fluctuations. The specific components of the indices (i.e. the economic indicators to include) depend on economic circumstances and how analysts measure the economy. Components can change over time. See Composite Leading Indicators (CLIs) in chapter 2.

Cyclical Variation

Cycles reflect short-term fluctuations around a longer-term trend. Cyclical variation in a dataset is a variation over a period of years. Business, economic, and trade cycles are good examples of this. For example, when considering GDP over a long period of time, there will be periods when growth jumps ahead and other periods when an economy is in recession. The cycle has four phases: expansion, peak, recession, and trough.

- Expansion – when demand begins to increase, it gathers momentum. The early sign is usually a run-down in stocks (inventories), and output begins to rise faster than demand while stocks are rebuilt. More workers are taken on and unemployment falls; more workers in employment means more consumer spending. This creates more demand, employment increases further as companies take on more staff, and the process continues. Eventually, producers reach their maximum capacity but if they are confident that demand will remain buoyant then they may invest in more plant and machinery.

- Peak – Eventually, output reaches a ceiling due to bottlenecks and supply constraints. For example, the economy may reach full employment with no more workers to take on or demand for investment funds may push up interest rates to the level where new investment is not profitable.

- Recession – As investment demand falls, producers of capital goods start to cut back on output and labour. Unemployment increases and consumer spending falls. The reverse of the expansion process begins to take place. In the US, a recession is defined as two consecutive quarters of falling GDP.

- Trough – Output will eventually stop falling at some minimum level (a trough) as many employees keep their jobs and spending power where they work in essential industries such as food, government, etc. Weak demand for investment funds will encourage interest rate falls and, eventually, investment will become an attractive option again.

Like Seasonal Variation (see that entry), cyclical variations can be removed from a dataset.

Data Mining

Data mining involves analysing data to try and identify interesting patterns in it. It is based on the use of software that looks for interesting or important patterns in data. It has mainly been used with internally generated data such as customer records, but it is applicable to other data sets. Software suppliers include leading IT companies such as IBM, Oracle, and SPSS.

Extrapolation

Extrapolation extends a trend identified in a time series over a specific period into the future, i.e. future trends are based on what has happened in recent years. This method has to be treated with some caution as there may be significant variations in the future which could affect the trend.

FOB

FOB (free on board) is the basis of the valuation of exports for customs purposes. It excludes the cost of insurance and freight from the country of assignment but includes all charges up to the point where goods are deposited on board export/import vessels or aircraft. Insurance and freight costs have to be added to be consistent with the valuation of imports, which is based on CIF (see that entry).

Forecasts

Forecasting is an analytical tool to aid decision-making and to provide evidence for future possibilities and scenarios under different given sets of conditions. The largest group of forecasts are economic, either macro-economic or micro-economic, and these forecasts can cover national, regional, or international areas. Other forecasts may examine likely future trends in specific industries, sectors, or markets.

Forecasts can be produced using different methodologies. The simplest are based on Extrapolation (see that entry) where predictions of future trends are based on current or recent trends. Some forecasts are based on surveys of managers and executives in specific countries or industries (see Opinion Polls and Business Surveys in chapter 5).

The more sophisticated forecasts use econometric models to predict future trends. Econometric models predict the future value of economic variables by examining other variables which are causally related to them. Econometric models link variables in the form of equations which can be estimated statistically and then used as a basis for forecasting. In complex economic situations, the independent variables in one equation are themselves influenced by other variables so that many equations may be necessary to represent all the causal relationships. The econometric model used by HM Treasury in the UK, for example, has around 600 equations.

Many econometric models were originally developed in the USA. The growth in UK forecasting took place in the 1970s when many organisations tried to deal with the economic consequences of the oil shocks in that decade. As there is an element of uncertainty in all forecasts, many forecasts often give a range of forecasts ranging from the most pessimistic scenario to the most optimistic.

Forecasts can cover different time periods although most forecasts usually only predict trends for a few years ahead at the most. Predicting trends over a longer period of time becomes even more problematic.

- Short term forecasts generally cover the next 12–18 months.
- Medium term forecasts may give figures up to 3–4 years ahead.
- Forecasts covering more than 4 years are long term forecasts.

Macro-economic forecasts typically cover such economic indicators as GDP, prices, employment, investment, and consumer spending. In the UK, over 30 organisations regularly produce forecasts and a good starting point is *Forecasts of the UK Economy*, published monthly by HM Treasury, which compares the forecasts from a selection of forecasters.

Growth Rates

Growth rates in published statistics can be expressed in a variety of ways and some of the most common are:

- Annual change – A comparison of the total or average for one calendar year, or other year such as fiscal, academic, or crop year, with the previous year. For example, sales were 4.6% higher in 2000 than in 1999.

- 12-month or 4-quarter change – A comparison of a specific month or quarter with the corresponding month or quarter in the previous year. For example, sales increased by 4.6% between the 2nd quarters of 2000 and 2001.

- Month-by-month or quarter-by-quarter change – A comparison of the latest month or quarter with the previous month or quarter. For example, sales in October 2000 were 4.6% higher than in September 2000.

- Annualised change – This is the change that would occur if the movement observed in any period were to continue for 12 months. For example, sales increased by 4.6% annualised during the first three quarters of 2000.

See also Compound Annual Growth Rate and Percentage Changes.

Index Numbers

Index numbers are measures designed to show changes in the value, price, quantity, or volume of a group of items over time. The aim of index numbers is to provide a way to simplify comparison over time. Any series of figures can be converted into an index and an index replaces complicated figures by simple ones calculated as percentages. Not only do index numbers allow quick comparisons to be made in one series of figures, but they are also helpful when comparing more than one series of figures.

An index is usually compiled by choosing a particular time period within a time series as the base year (see Base Year) and then expressing changes in subsequent or previous time periods as percentage changes over the base time period.

Using GDP value figures at current prices for France, Germany, Italy, and the UK, the example below describes the calculation of an index and shows its usefulness. Comparing annual GDP growth in France, Germany, and the UK between 1997 and 1999 and working out which country has experienced the fastest growth is difficult with GDP value figures as each country's GDP may be expressed in national currencies and it is not immediately clear from the three sets of figures what the level of GDP growth is in each country, and which GDP is growing at the fastest rate.

GDP value at current prices in national currencies, 1997–1999

	France (FFrbn)	Germany (DMbn)	Italy (L000bn)	UK (£bn)
1997	8,207.1	3,666.5	1,983.9	805.40
1998	8,536.3	3,784.4	2,067.7	851.65
1999	8,823.8	3,877.2	2,128.2	891.00

Source: OECD Main Economic Indicators

To convert the above series into index figures, a year is chosen as the base year and this year is given an index value of 100. In this example, 1997 is chosen as the base year but, in a longer time series, any year could be chosen. The index for every country starts at 100 in 1997. Using France as an example, the 1998 and 1999 GDP value figures will now be converted into an index:

In 1998, the value of GDP in France was 8,536.3 compared with 8,207.1 in 1997, the base year. The difference between 1998 and 1997 in value terms is 329.2, i.e. 8,536.3 – 8,207.1. The 329.2 figure represents the growth in GDP in 1998 compared with 1997. This growth must be calculated as a percentage growth over the base year value in 1997. The calculation is:

329.2 divided by 8,207.1 (base year value) multiplied by 100 = 4.0

Therefore, the percentage growth in GDP in 1998 over the base year (1997) was 4.0% and to express this as an index, 4 is added to the base year figure of 100 to produce 104.0 for GDP growth in 1998.

A similar exercise is carried out for 1999 remembering that GDP growth in 1999 is related to the base year (1997) and not the previous year (1998). In 1999, the value of GDP was 8,823.8 and the difference between the 1999 value and the 1997 value was 616.7. The 616.7 represents the growth in GDP in 1999 compared with 1997. Again, this growth must be calculated as percentage growth over the base year value in 1997. The calculation is:

616.7 divided by 8,207.1 (base year value) multiplied by 100 = 7.5

Therefore, the percentage growth in GDP in 1999 over the base year (1997) was 7.5% and to express this as an index, 7.5 is added to the base year figure of 100 to produce 107.5 for GDP growth in 1999.

If similar calculations are carried out for the three other countries then the table below is produced. This shows clearly that the strongest growth in GDP between 1997 and 1999 has been in the UK with the GDP index increasing from 100 in 1997 to 110.6 in 1999. The weakest growth was in Germany where the index increased from 100 in 1997 to 105.7 in 1999.

Index of GDP value at current prices (1997 = 100), 1997–99

	France	Germany	Italy	UK
1997	100.0	100.0	100.0	100.0
1998	104.0	103.2	104.2	105.7
1999	107.5	105.7	107.3	110.6

As well as measuring growth, index numbers can also indicate decreases in value or volumes. For example, if in the above example 1998 had been used as the base year instead of 1997 then the following index numbers would have been produced:

Index of GDP value at current prices (1998 = –100), 1997–99

	France	Germany	Italy	UK
1997	96.1	96.9	96.0	94.6
1998	100.0	100.0	100.0	100.0
1999	103.4	102.5	102.9	104.6

The 1999 index figures are based on the same calculation as described above. The 1997 index figures are calculated by subtracting the 1997 value figure from the 1998 (base year) figure. For France, this produces a value figure of 329.2. Again, this is calculated as a percentage of the value in the base year but instead of adding the result to 100, the final figure is subtracted from a 100 to produce the index number:

329.2 divided by 8,536.3 (base year value) multiplied by 100 = 3.9

Subtracting 3.9 from a 100 produces an index figure for 1997 of 96.1 for France.

Many well-established statistical indicators are published as indexes and some examples include the retail price's index (RPI), the Index of

Industrial Production (IOP), and the Retail Sales Index. The base years for these published indexes are usually changed every 15–20 years.

Two or more indices can be combined to form one composite index. For example, indices of household spending on specific products can all be combined to produce one index of household spending. The simplest way of combining indices is to calculate a weighted average using the same weights throughout. This is referred to as a base-weighted index, or a Laspeyres index (named after the German economist who developed it). Here is an example of a base-weighted price index for household consumption of wine and milk per week:

Product	Price (£)		Quantity consumed (litres)	
	1995	2000	1995	2000
Wine	9	11	5	6
Milk	5	8	3	3

Weekly household expenditure in 1995:

> = 1995 quantity of wine × 1995 price of wine
> + 1995 quantity of milk × 1995 price of milk
> = 5 × 9 + 3 × 5
> = 45.0 + 15.0 = 60.0

Weekly expenditure in 2000, based on 1995 quantities:

> = 1995 quantity of wine × 2000 price of wine
> + 1995 quantity of cheese × 2000 price of cheese
> = 5 × 11 + 3 × 8
> = 55.0 + 24.0 = 79.0

Index number for 1995 = 60.0/60.0 × 100 = 100.0

Index number for 2000 = 79.0/60.0 × 100 = 131.7

Where weighted averages are used, the weights usually need revising from time to time. With the retail price's index (RPI) for example, spending patterns change over time due to relative cost, quality, availability, new delivery channels, etc. One way to try and deal with this is to calculate a new set of current weights at regular intervals and use these to derive a single long-term index. This is referred to as a current-weighted index, or a Paasche index (again named after the originator). Here is an example of a current weighted price index for the household consumption of wine and milk per week:

Product	Price (£)		Quantity consumed (litres)	
	1995	2000	1995	2000
Wine	9	11	5	6
Milk	5	8	3	3

Weekly expenditure in 1995, based on 2000 quantities

$= 2000$ quantity of wine $\times$ 1995 price of wine

$+ 2000$ quantity of milk $\times$ 1995 price of milk

$= 6 \times 9 + 3 \times 5$

$= 54.0 + 15.0 = 69.0$

Weekly expenditure in 2000

$= 2000$ quantity of wine $\times$ 2000 price of wine

$+ 2000$ quantity of milk $\times$ 2000 price of milk

$= 6 \times 11 + 3 \times 8$

$= 66.0 + 24.0 = 90.0$

Index number for 1995 $= 69.0/69.0 \times 100 = 100.0$

Index number for 2000 $= 90.0/69.0 \times 100 = 130.4$

Base-weighted indices are relatively simple to calculate but they tend to overstate changes over time. Current-weighted indices are more complicated to calculate and can understate long-term changes.

There is no ideal way of weighting indices and often indices are a combination of both base-weighting and current-weighting. In published indices, a new set of weights is normally introduced every 5, 10, or 15 years and, when this happens, a new base year and new index is created which has to be 'chained' to the previous index to maintain the series and produce comparisons over long time periods. There is a relatively straightforward calculation involved in the chaining of indices and all that is required is that one period is covered by both indices.

The example in the table below shows that the year 1998 is covered by both indices. The calculation to create a chained index is as follows:

- For 1998, divide the new figure by the old figure, $83/133 = 0.62$

- Multiply all the figures in the old index by the above result, i.e. each figure in column 1 multiplied by 0.62 produces the figures in column 3

- Add the rebased figures in column 3 to the new index figures to create the chained index.

Chaining Index Numbers

	Old index	New index	Old index rebased	Chained index
1	2	3	4	
1995	100		62	62
1996	110		68	68
1997	121		75	75
1998	133	83	83	83
1999		91		91
2000		100		100
2001		110		110

Like-for-like Statistics

Like-for-like statistics compare variables in one period with the same variables in another period, and avoid any changes in data which have been caused by changes in the population being surveyed. For example, a retail chain might have 300 outlets in year 1 but this increases to 320 outlets in year 2. Comparing total sales in year 2 with year 1 is not comparing like with like as there are 20 more outlets in year 2. Like-for-like sales would compare sales from the 300 outlets in year 1 with these same outlets in year 2.

Manufacturer's Selling Prices

Values in a time series are expressed in the prices obtained by manufacturers of materials and products.

Measures of Central Tendency

Measures of central tendency show the grouping together of the figures around some central point of data. This usually involves working out an average and the amount of variation around the average.

Averages
- The *arithmetic mean* is the sum of the readings, or units recorded in a survey, divided by the number of readings or units recorded. This is easily calculated but it can be misleading if the results contain some atypically high or low values.
- The *median* is the half way point in a set of results or readings. It is unaffected by extreme results.

- The *mode* is the most frequently occurring value in a set of results or readings. The mode is also unaffected by extreme results and is a good representation of the 'typical' value

The *arithmetic mean* is the most often used. However, the mode and mean can be useful descriptions with peculiar frequency distributions. Counting the number of times each value occurs in a set of readings provides a frequency distribution.

Measures of Dispersion

Measures of dispersion measure the variability of the data in survey results, i.e. how great is the range of the figures.

The *range* is the simplest method and this calculates the range of readings or results by subtracting the lowest value in a distribution from the highest.

Another method is to divide any distribution into a series of four equal parts. The points marking the division between these parts are known as *quartiles*. The interquartile range is the difference between the upper quartile and the lower quartile. If the upper and lower 25% of the distribution (upper and lower quartiles) are excluded then any extreme values will not skew the data. We are left with the interquartile range and what is being measured is the spread of the middle 50% of the distribution. A distribution can also be divided into other equal parts, for example quintiles which divide any distribution into five equal parts (20% each of the distribution) or deciles which divide a distribution into 10 equal parts (10% each of the distribution).

The main weakness when using either the range or the interquartile range is that neither measure of dispersion uses all the values in a distribution. The *standard deviation* uses all the values in a distribution and shows the dispersion of these values around the arithmetic mean. The greater the dispersion, the larger the standard deviation. To calculate the standard deviation, the deviation of each value from the arithmetic mean is taken and then an average is calculated from these deviations.

Metadata

Metadata is best described as data about data. Metadata includes user guides, support material, and other documentation which accompanies any statistics and provides information and explanation about these statistics.

Minimum Threshold

In many UK government business surveys, samples are taken from companies and enterprises above a certain size or above a minimum threshold. These minimum thresholds are often based on employment size and can vary from sector to sector. While companies or enterprises below this minimum threshold are not included in any samples, estimates are often made for these companies or enterprises to provide a more complete picture of the sector.

Moving Annual Total

A moving annual total (MAT) figure is sometimes used in time series with monthly or quarterly data. The MAT usually refers to the annual figure up to the latest date published. For example, if the latest published statistics refer to August 2000 then the MAT is the figure for the year up to the end of August 2000.

Moving Average

A moving average is a series of arithmetic means calculated from data in a time series which reduces the effects of seasonal variations.

Net Supply

Net supply is a term used in UK official statistics to show how much of a specific product is supplied to the UK market in a particular time period. It is calculated by taking a figure for UK manufacturer's sales of a product (i.e. total sales by UK suppliers), subtracting exports and adding imports. The final figure from the calculation is the net supply figure.

The net supply calculation offers a guide to the size of a specific market or product sector in the absence of any market size figures produced from other sources.

Bear in mind that the net supply figure can be negative. This can happen when there has been considerable re-exporting of imported goods, or where there are significant exports of stockpiled goods which were manufactured in a previous time period.

Net supply figures are published in *Product Sales* and *Trade* publications (see PRODCOM Inquiry in chapter 6). An example of the calculation is:

UK net supply of safety or relief valves

Quarter 2, Year 2000	£000
UK manufacturers sales	15,653
Less exports	9,213
=	6,440
Plus imports	10,991
=	17,431
UK net supply	17,431

Source: Product Sales and Trade PRQ33, Taps and Valves

In the above example, value figures are used but the same calculation can be used with volume figures, e.g. tonnes, kilograms, number of units, etc.

Another term – UK apparent consumption – is also used in some statistical publications and survey reports to express the same meaning as UK net supply and the same calculation as above is used.

Non-governmental Statistics

Non-governmental statistics, sometimes referred to as unofficial statistics, are statistics collected, processed, and produced by non-governmental organisations and agencies. Although central government is a major producer of statistics in most developed countries, other important producers of statistics include trade associations and professional bodies, banks and other financial services companies, chambers of commerce and local development agencies, research companies, publishers, and academic institutions.

Official Statistics

Official statistics, sometimes referred to as governmental statistics, is the terminology used to describe all those statistics collected, processed, and produced by central government and central government departments and agencies. This official data is often published by a national statistical office or agency. See also Non-governmental Statistics.

Percentage Calculations

There are various percentage calculations that can be done relatively easily from published statistics and using a calculator. A few examples are given below.

Finding one number as a percentage of another
140 as a percentage of 180 is calculated by dividing 140 by 180 (140/ 180 = 0.77) and then multiplying the answer by 100 (0.77 ∞ 100 = 77.7%).

Finding the percentage change between two amounts
What is the change between 110 and 150 expressed as a percentage of 110? Divide 150 by 110 (150/110 = 1.36), then take 1 away from the answer (1.36 − 1 = 0.36), and multiply the answer by 100 (0.36 ∞ 100 = 36%).

Another way of calculating this is to subtract 110 from 150 (150 − 110 = 40), then calculate 40 as a percentage of 110 (as the previous example, this produces the result of 36.3%, or 36% to the nearest whole number).

Finding an amount after a given percentage increase or decrease
If 120 increased by 25%, what did it increase to? Start by dividing 25 by 100 (25/100 = 0.25), add 1 to the result (0.25 + 1 = 1.25), then multiply the original number by 1.25 (1.25 ∞ 120 = 150). 150 is 25% greater than 120.

Percentage Changes

Percentage points are not the same as percentage changes. For example, if retail prices increase from 10% to 14% over a period time, these prices have risen by four units, or four percentage points. However, the percentage increase has been 40%, 4 divided by 10 ∞ 100. See also Percentage Calculations.

Provisional Figures

The first, preliminary, or most important results of some surveys and statistical calculations are published as provisional figures but many of these figures are later revised when more data is available for analysis. Economic data such as quarterly GDP estimates or monthly balance of trade figures are published quickly to allow for up-to-date economic analysis and monitoring but these figures are often based on incomplete data and analysis. Many of these provisional figures are likely to be revised at a subsequent date and some figures can be revised on more than one occasion.

National Statistics *First Releases* and many press releases and statistical bulletins containing official statistics have provisional data.

Random Variation

Random variation in a time series is impossible to control. Sometimes called 'catastrophic variation', it can be caused by many factors which are usually unforeseen. For example, freak weather conditions might affect the production figures for a particular foodstuff.

Ratios

Ratios are used to express the relationship between two sets of figures. One figure is often expressed as a percentage of another figure. For example, the export sales ratio shows the percentage of UK manufacturer's sales that are exported.

Recession

A recession in an economy is usually characterised by falling GDP, increasing unemployment, and falling consumer spending. There are some technical definitions of a recession used by statisticians in certain countries. In the US, for example, a recession is defined as two consecutive quarters of falling GDP. The problem with this definition is that if GDP falls dramatically in the first and third quarters of a year, but rises in the second and fourth quarters, this is not technically a recession according to the above definition although output may be considerably lower at the end of the year than it was at the beginning. Another definition states that a recession is a year-on-year fall in output.

Retail Selling Prices

Values in a time series expressed at retail selling prices (RSP) are based on the retail prices of goods and services. This is particularly applicable to consumer goods and services sold through retail outlets and other retail channels.

Revised Figures

The first results of some surveys and statistical calculations are published as provisional figures but these are later revised when more data is available for analysis. Economic data such as quarterly GDP estimates or monthly balance of trade figures are published quickly to allow for up-to-date economic analysis and monitoring but these provisional figures are often based on incomplete data and analysis. Many of these provisional figures are likely to be revised at a subsequent date and some figures can be revised on more than one occasion.

In particular, economic data in National Statistics *First Releases*, which is published quickly, may be revised later in other publications such as *Economic Trends* or *Financial Statistics*. Users should treat these *First Releases* as press releases and earlier issues of these releases should be ignored when checking historical data particularly if there is access to sources likely to contain revised data such as *Economic Trends* and *Financial Statistics*.

Rounding Figures

In some published time series, to simplify the published data if it includes decimal points the figures are rounded. The usual convention in rounding figures is that 5 and over are rounded up to the next figure, and 4 and under are rounded down to the lower figure. For example, 7.5 would be rounded up to 8 while 7.4 would be rounded down to 7.0. Bear in mind that there are 10 divisions in a figure and 5 is not the middle number:

0,1,2,3,4 5,6,7,8,9

With more complicated numbers and if the decimal point is to be retained, rounding can be used to simplify the data after the decimal point. The same convention applies: for example, 7.37 becomes 7.4 and 7.32 becomes 7.3.

Sampling

A sample is a selection from a given set or population of items. The purpose of a sample is generally to save time, effort and money dealing with a sub-group rather than the whole population. But it is a matter of economics. A sample can never tell us more than if we had measured the whole population.

To be useful, a sample must be representative of the population from which it was selected, at least to some degree of close approximation. There is always some loss of precision in dealing with a sample, but this may be acceptable if the amount of error is known.

The theory and practice of random sampling ensures that one knows how close the sample is likely to be to the population. The size and cost implications of possible sampling errors have to be balanced against data collection and analysis. The safe way to take a sample is by random sampling or some other statistical method. Statistical sampling is required when there is substantial and largely unpredictable variability in the population.

Random sampling
Random sampling means that every item in the population to be surveyed has an equal chance of selection for the sample. A more sophisticated form of random sampling is stratified random sampling where the study population is grouped according to meaningful characteristics of strata, e.g. men/women; age bands; mature students/ other students; postgraduate/undergraduate. Random samples are taken within each strata.

Random sampling is the most statistically reliable way of creating a sample, but there are other forms of sampling such as:

Convenience sampling
Use of a group of individuals or units that is readily available, e.g. patients in a waiting room.

Selecting the first items from a list
It must be known beforehand that the order of the list is not related to whatever we are measuring.

Systematic sampling
Taking every nth item (e.g. 1 in 10). *Systematic sampling* is merely a cost cutting device to avoid the extra fuss and cost of random sampling.

Quota sampling
The population is divided into subgroups, e.g. male students living on a college campus, female students living on a college campus, male students living in lodgings, female students living in lodgings. A sample is selected based on the proportions of subgroups needed to represent the proportions in the population.

Seasonal Variation

Seasonal variation is a seasonal change in a dataset which can usually be predicted as it occurs on a regular basis. For example: retail sales figures always increase in the period before Christmas because consumers are spending more on gifts and food; employment in tourism-related industries increases in the summer months.

Where seasonal variations are a feature of a dataset, seasonally adjusted figures are usually published alongside non-seasonally adjusted figures. Non-seasonally adjusted figures simply publish the basic data for each time period. By averaging seasonal influences from the original dataset, seasonally adjusted figures in a time series remove the regular variation and provide a clearer picture of long term trends. See Moving Averages.

Seasonally Adjusted Figures

See Seasonal Variation.

Standard Deviation

See Measures of Dispersion.

Standard Error

The standard error is a measure of the degree to which an estimate based on a sample may differ from the true value because the sample used is only of limited size.

Statistical Confidence

The reliability of results from statistical surveys is based on assessing the statistical confidence in various responses at different levels of sample size. Survey estimates from random samples have the mathematical property that a known proportion of values lies beyond certain multiples of the standard error (see Standard Error):

- 95% of values are within the range of arithmetic mean ±1.96 standard errors and only 5% are outside

- 99% of values are within the range of arithmetic mean ±2.58 standard errors and only 1% are outside.

Survey data is usually reported at these two levels of confidence. For example, the 95% confidence level means that we are 95% confident that the values lie within the stated limits for every 19 out of 20 sample surveys we might carry out in a given population. For the 99% level, we are 99% confident that the values lie within the stated limits for every 99 out of 100 sample surveys we might carry out in a given population.

Trends

Change from one time period to the next. Trend analysis evaluates these changes.

Time Series

Time series are datasets containing data gathered over a period of time (e.g. weekly, daily, monthly, annually, etc.). Trend analysis considers how the data varies over time.

Unofficial Statistics

See Non-governmental Statistics.

Year-on-Year Data

One year's figures compared with the previous year's figures. Sometimes used across a series of years if the trend has been the same throughout these years. For example, the catering industry has experienced year-on-year increases in sales at current prices over the last five years.

Appendix 1

Abbreviations and acronyms

ABI	Annual Business Inquiry
ACORN	A Classification of Residential Neighbourhoods
AEI	Average Earnings Index
AES	Annual Employment Survey
ANCOM	Andean Common Market
APEC	Asian-Pacific Economic Cooperation
ASEAN	Association of South-East Asian Nations
BARB	Broadcasters Audience Research Board
BGEI	Solomon Smith Barney Global Equity Indices
BHPS	British Household Panel Survey
BMI	Body Mass Index
BMRB	British Market Research Bureau
BMRC	British Media Research Committee
BoE	Bank of England
BOP	Balance of Payments
BSUG	Business Statistics Users' Group
CAAGR	Compound Average Annual Growth Rate
CACEU	Central African Customs and Economic Union
CACM	Central American Common Market
CARICOM	Caribbean Community and Common Market
CBI	Confederation of British Industry
CC	Classification of Types of Construction
CCCN	Customs Cooperation Council Nomenclature
CCIs	Composite Cyclical Indicators
CED	Consumers' Expenditure Deflator

CEETE	Central and Eastern European Transition Economies
CIF	cost of insurance and freight
CIS	Commonwealth of Independent States
CJSF	Criminal Justice Statistics Forum
CLI	Composite Leading Indicator
CN	Combined Nomenclature
COFOG	Classification of the Functions of Government
COICOP	Classification of Individual Consumption by Purpose
COMESA	Common Market for Eastern and Southern Africa
COMEXT	Eurostat's external trade database
COMTRADE	Commodity Trade Database
COPNI	Classification of the Purposes of Non-Profit Institutions serving Households
COPP	Classification of the Outlays of Producers by Purpose
CPA	Statistical Classification of Products by Activity in the European Economic Community
CPI	Consumer Price Index
CRR	Composite Risk Rating
CSPI	Corporate Services Price Index
DEFRA	Department of the Environment, Food and Rural Affairs
DFES	Department for Education and Skills
DTI	Department of Trade and Industry
DTLR	Department of Transport, Local Government and the Regions
DWP	Department for Work and Pensions
ECE	United Nations Economic Commission for Europe
ECHPS	European Commission Household Panel Survey
ECHS	English House Condition Survey
ECOWAS	Economic Community of West African States
ECU	European Currency Unit
ED	Enumeration District
EEA	European Economic Area
EFS	Expenditure and Food Survey

EFTA	European Free Trade Association
EMIC	Export Marketing Information Centre (now replaced by Trade Partners UK Information Centre)
EMS	European Monetary System
EMU	Economic and Monetary Union
ER	Economic Rating
ERI	Exchange Rate Index
ESA	European System of Integrated Economic Accounts
ESSPROS	European System of Integrated Social Protection Statistics
e-TPI	e-Tail Price Index
ETSUG	Education and Training Statistics Users' Group
EU	European Union
EUROPROMS	Eurostat's product database
EUROSTAT	Statistical Office of the European Communities
FAO	Food and Agricultural Organisation
FEPI	Final Expenditure Prices Index
FES	Family Expenditure Survey
FMCG	Fast Moving Consumer Good
FOB	free on board
FR	financial rating
FRS	Family Resources Survey
FSUG	Financial Statistics Users' Group
FTV	Film and Television Survey
G7	Group of Seven
GAD	Government Actuary's Department
GATT	General Agreement on Tariffs and Trade
GDP	Gross Domestic Product
GDP(E)	Gross Domestic Product – Expenditure
GDP(I)	Gross Domestic Product – Income
GDP(O)	Gross Domestic Product – Output
GERD	Gross Expenditure on Research & Development
GHS	General Household Survey

GNI	Gross National Income
GNP	Gross National Product
GOR	Government Office Region
GRO	General Registry Office
GSS	Government Statistical Service
GWP	Gross World Product
HBAI	Households Below Average Income
HESA	Higher Education Statistics Agency
HICP	Harmonised Indices of Consumer Prices
HS	Harmonised Commodity Description and Coding System
HSE	Health Survey for England
HSUG	Health Statistics User Group
ICD	International Classification of Diseases
ICN	Intrastat Classification Nomenclature
ICRG	International Country Risk Guide
IDBR	Inter-Departmental Business Register
IEA	International Energy Agency
IFS	International Financial Statistics
IGP	Index of Government Prices
IIP	Index of Investment Prices
ILO	International Labour Organisation
IMF	International Monetary Fund
IOP	Index of Industrial Production
IOS	Index of Services
IOT	Input–Output Tables
IPS	International Passenger Survey
IR	Inland Revenue
ISCE	International Standard Classification of Status in Employment
ISCED	International Standard Classification of Education
ISCO	International Standard Classification of Occupations
ISIC	International Standard Industrial Classification

ITIS	International Trade in Services Survey
ITSUG	International Trade Statistics Users' Group
JICPOPS	Joint Industry Committee for Population Standards
JICREG	Joint Industry Committee for Regional Press Research
KAU	Kind of Activity Unit
LABORSTA	Labour Statistics Database from the International Labour Organisation
LAIA	Latin American Integration Association
LATW	Learning and Training at Work Survey
LDCs	Least Developed Countries
LFS	Labour Force Survey
LMSUG	Labour Market Statistics Users' Group
LS	Longitudinal Study
MAFF	Ministry of Agriculture Fisheries and Food
MAT	Moving Annual Total
MERCOSUR	Mercado Común Sudamericano
MLR	minimum lending rate
MSCI	Morgan Stanley Capital International
MSI	Monthly Sales Inquiry
MSP	Manufacturers' Selling Prices
N.C.E.	Used in statistical tables to denote 'not covered else where'
NACE	Nomenclature Générale des Activités Économiques dans les Communautés Européennes
NAF	Nomenclature des Activités Françaises
NAFTA	North American Free Trade Area
NAUG	National Accounts Users' Group
NDI	National Disposable Income
NDNS	National Diet and Nutrition Survey
NEDO	National Economic Development Office
NES	New Earnings Survey
NFS	National Food Survey
NHS	National Health Service

NIMEXE	Nomenclature of Goods for the External Trade Statistics of the Community and Statistics of Trade between Member States
NOMIS	National Online Manpower Information System
NRS	National Readership Survey
NS	National Statistics
NSILS	National Statistics Information and Library Service
NS-SEC	National Statistics Socio-Economic Classification
NTS	National Travel Survey
NUTS	Nomenclature of Territorial Units for Statistics
NYSE	New York Stock Exchange
OECD	Organisation for Economic Cooperation and Development
ONS	Office for National Statistics
OPEC	Organisation of Petroleum Exporting Countries
OTS	Overseas Trade Statistics
PACSTAT	Production and Construction Statistics
PARIS21	Partnership in Statistics for Development in the 21st Century
PAYE	Pay As Your Earn
PDF	Portable Document Format (Adobe Acrobat files)
PDI	Personal Disposable Income
PPI	Producer Prices Index
POSTAR	Poster Advertising Research
PPP	Purchasing Power Parity
PRODCOM	PRODucts of the European COMmunity
PRS	Political Risk Services
PSBR	Public Sector Borrowing Requirement
PSDR	Public Sector Debt Repayment
QOLC	Quality of Life Counts
RAJAR	Radio Joint Audience Research
RCADE	Resource Centre for Access to Data on Europe
REGIO	Eurostat's regional statistics database

ROI	Redistribution of Income
RPDI	Real Personal Disposable Income
RPI	Retail Prices Index
RSI	Retail Sales Index
RSP	Retail Selling Prices
S&P	Standard & Poor's
SAS	Small Area Statistics
SDR	Unit of Account for the International Monetary Fund
SEC	Socio-Economic Classification
SIC	Standard Industrial Classification
SITC	Standard International Trade Classification
SNA	System of National Accounts
SOC	Standard Occupational Classification
SS-BGEI	Solomon Smith Barney Global Equity Indices
SSR	Standard Statistical Region
STAN	STructural ANalysis Industrial Database
SUC	Statistics Users' Council
TGI	Target Group Index
TOPIX	Tokyo Stock Price Index
TPI	Tax and Price Index
TRAIN	TRade Analysis and INformation System
TSUG	Transport Statistics Users' Group
UN	United Nations
UN/ECE	United Nations Economic Commission for Europe
UNCTAD	United Nations Conference on Trade and Development
UNESCO	United Nations Educational, Scientific and Cultural Organisation
UNIDO	United Nations Industrial Development Organisation
URL	Uniform Resource Locator (Internet address)
VAT	Value Added Tax
WDI	World Development Indicator
WEI	World Education Indicator

WPI	Wholesale Price Index
WTO	World Trade Organisation

Appendix 2

Selected Web sites

UK

www.bankofengland.co.uk
The Bank of England's Web site has free access to various monetary statistics.

www.culture.gov.uk
Free basic data on culture, sports, and the media in the UK.

www.data-archive.ac.uk
The Web site of the data archive at the University of Essex.

www.defra.gov.uk
The Web site of the Department for Environment, Food and Rural Affairs has replaced the MAFF site and has free access to statistics.

www.dfes.gov.uk
The Web site of the Department for Education and Skills with details of education statistics plus access to many data sets.

www.dltr.gov.uk
The Web site of the Department of Transport, Local Government and the Regions has free statistics pages with official statistics covering planning and land use, housing, and transport.

www.doh.gov.uk
Details of health statistics, data from surveys and statistical releases are freely available.

www.dti.gov.uk
The Department of Industry's Web site has some press releases with statistics and other surveys.

www.dwp.gov.uk
Various statistics and statistical releases on the Department for Work and Pensions Web site.

www.gad.gov.uk
The Web site of the Government Actuary's Department has details of population projections and life tables plus access to the latest projections.

www.gro-scotland.gov.uk
The Web site of the General Registry Office in Scotland with free access to population data.

www.hm-treasury.gov.uk
Some free economic indicators and economic overviews on the Web site.

www.inlandrevenue.gov.uk
The Inland Revenue Web site has free access to statistical series and surveys.

www.ndad.ulcc.ac.uk
The web site of the National Digital Archive of Datasets. Open access to government datasets.

www.nisra.gov.uk
The Web site of the Northern Ireland Statistics and Research Agency.

www.statistics.gov.uk
The Web site for UK national statistics with free access to data through Statbase, pages for specific titles, and downloadable files.

www.wales.gov.uk
Access to Welsh statistics and other publications on site.

International

www.europa.eu.int/comm/eurostat
The Web site of Eurostat with free key indicators and statistical summaries plus details of titles, services, and Data Shops.

www.fao.org
Access to a range of international and country-specific agricultural, forestry, food, and fishing statistics on the Web site.

www.iea.org
The Web site of the International Energy Agency has free access to various energy statistics.

www.ilo.org
The Web site of the International Labour Organisation offers free access to LABORSTA, its labour statistics database, with detailed data on labour markets in various countries.

www.imf.org
The IMF Web site offers some free access to IMF reports and economic reviews.

www.lib.umich.edu/govdocs/stats.html
Maintained by the University of Michigan, the site has details of international statistics arranged by subject. Updated regularly.

www.ntu.edu.sg/library/stat/statdata.htm
Links to international statistical publications and sources arranged by geographical area. The site is only updated infrequently.

www.oecd.org/statistics
There are some basic statistics on the site plus details of all surveys, publications, and statistical services.

www.popnet.org
A source of world population data and demographic information.

www.unctad.org
Details of statistics and some free access to international trade data.

www.unece.org
The Web site of the United Nations Economic Commission for Europe (UNECE) with details of statistical programmes and publications, plus free summary data by country.

www.unesco.org
Details of statistics and publications and some free access to data.

www.un.org/depts/unsd
Some statistics plus details of services and publications.

www.worldbank.org
The World Bank Web site has free access to economic and social data on various countries.

www.wto.org
Web site of the World Trade Organisation, the successor to GATT, with details of statistics and methodologies.

Appendix 3

Statistics users' councils and statistics user groups

Business Statistics Users' Group (BSUG)

Secretary: Geoff Noon. Email: *gnoon@mtta.co.uk*

Criminal Justice Statistics Forum (CJSF)

Secretary: Gordon Barclay. Email: *Gordon.Barclay@homeoffice.gsi.gov.uk*

Education and Training Statistics Users' Group (ETSUG)

Secretary: Brian A Clegg. Email: *brian.clegg@mail.nasuwt.org.uk*

Financial Statistics Users' Group (FSUG)

Secretary: Daxa Khilosia. Tel: 020 7601 5353

Gender Statistics Users' Group

Secretary: Dr Karen Hurrell. Email: *Karen.hurrell@eoc.org.uk*

Health Statistics User Group (HSUG)

Secretary: Seán Boyle. Email: *rescue_uk@yahoo.com*

International Trade Statistics Users' Group (INTRASTAT/ITSUG)

Secretary: Kristina Lawson. Email: *klawson@tarrc.co.uk*

Labour Market Statistics Users' Group (LMSUG)

Secretary: David Taylor. Email: *david.taylor@btinternet.com*

National Accounts Users' Group (NAUG)

Secretary: Jon Beadle. Email: *jon.beadle@ons.gov.uk*

Statistics Users' Council (SUC)

Secretary: Duncan McKenzie. Email: *d.mckenzie@ifsl.org.uk*

Transport Statistics Users' Group (TSUG)

Secretary: Fred Hitchins. Email: *fred@irn-research.com*